Y0-CBB-510

CLASSIC VINTAGE
Nose Art

Gary M. Valant

Lowe & B. Hould
Publishers

This edition published in 1997 by Lowe and B. Hould, an imprint of Borders, Inc., 515 East Liberty, Ann Arbor, MI 48104
Lowe & B. Hould Publishers is a trademark of Borders Properties, Inc.

This edition first published in 1987 by Motorbooks International Publishers & Wholesalers, 729 Prospect Ave, PO Box 1, Osceola, WI 54020-0001 USA

© Gary Valant, 1987

All rights reserved. With the exception of quoting brief passages for the purposes of review no part of this publication may be reproduced without prior written permission from the Publisher

Motorbooks International is a certified trademark, registered with the United States Patent Office

The information in this book is true and complete to the best of our knowledge. All recommendations are made without any guarantee on the part of the author or Publisher, who also disclaim any liability incurred in connection with the use of this data or specific details

We recognize that some words, model names and designations, for example, mentioned herein are the property of the trademark holder. We use them for identification purposes only. This is not an official publication

Library of Congress Cataloging-in-Publication Data Available

ISBN 0-681-22744-3

Printed in Hong Kong

Contents

Dedication

This book is dedicated to all of the air crews whose humor and imagination decorated World War II combat aircraft, and to those who strive to preserve the great history and aircraft of that era.

My special thanks to the following people.

Clarence Simonsen of Alberta, Canada, who supplied many of the very hard to find color photos and related information. Clarence has been interested in aircraft for as long as he can remember, and has been collecting nose art since the 1960s. He has written many articles and has had a nose art column in the *Eighth Air Force News*.

Paul M. Andrews of Vienna, Virginia, has been invaluable in the identification of the Eighth Air Force nose art. He is currently working on a compilation of the combat missions of the 95th Bomb Group that will be incorporated into their unit history, and has also written a number of articles about the Eighth Air Force.

Robert Mann for his assistance on the 19th and 98th Bomb Group B-29s.

Antony Giacobbe for his nose art files and contacts.

Tim Bivens for all of his contributions.

Leland "Pappy" Martin of the Confederate Air Force, along with Tony and Javier, who spent the night moving all of that equipment around the hangar while I photographed the nose art hanging on the walls.

Melissa Keiser of the National Air and Space Museum for all of her assistance before and during our visit.

The fine staff at the US Air Force Museum, Dayton, Ohio.

Everyone else who sent information or photographs in support of this book.

The crew and unit commander of USAF F-111 "Lucky Strike," whose nose art got me interested in doing this book.

And last, but not least, my family: Nancy, Bonnie and Michael, who gave me so much help and support on this project.

Preface

It's mid-winter 1943, you're twenty years old, it's 04:30 in the morning, it's raining, it's cold. You've got a slight hangover, and you're walking in mud (there's always mud).

You're wearing a fur-lined flying suit, because where you're going it's thirty degrees below zero. You've got an oxygen mask, because where you're going it's hard to breathe. You're carrying a map, because at 25,000 feet there are no signs. Prior to December 7, 1941, your main goal in life was to get a car and marry Ginger Rogers, but now it's just to stay alive another day, because you're a crewman on a B-17, and where you're going, people are going to die.

But not *you*, not *your* plane, not *your* crew, because you're special, and the special people always come back. They don't blow up in the sky, or go in at 400 miles per hour, one wing gone, no chutes, on fire—not the special ones; they always come back.

So we need a special name for our plane— and a special picture on it. Maybe a picture of Betty Grable, or one of those Vargas girls from *Esquire.* And we'll name it something like "Sack Time," "Mister Completely" or "Target For Tonight." But it has to be special, and when it's finished, it will be ready—
Ready for Duty.

Introduction

It was good or it was bad, it was naughty or nice, funny or sad, and sometimes it was self-deprecating, and during World War II it was everywhere. It has come to be known as *nose art*, because it was normally found on or about the nose of the aircraft.

The origin of nose art goes back to some ancient time when the first proud charioteer decorated his vehicle so that it would be distinguishable from the others. The desire to personalize an object, a machine, to make it unique among the multitude, is basic to man's nature. Place man under great stresses, give him a very uncertain future, and this desire can become an obsession. So it is in war, and with the machines of war. A thousand B-17s, identical in every way, roll off the assembly line and fly to an uncertain fate, but each one can be different. The difference is not in the tail number. Those are for record keepers and ribbon clerks. The difference is in the imagination and talent of the crew. Few crew members would talk about 247613 or 34356, but many tales would be told about "Sack Time" or "The Dragon Lady."

The ideas for nose art came from everywhere; girlfriends, wives, posters, matchbook covers, calendars, the comics or some event related to the history of the aircraft. The "Swamp Angel" landed in a swamp, "Patched Up Piece" had probably been repaired more than once. "Just Once More" seems like a reasonable request for a B-17 crew trying to complete twenty-five missions so they could go home. "Better Duck" could have two meanings, and "SHEDONWANNA?" could relate to problems that the crew had with the aircraft.

But the majority of the nose art was inspired by the artwork in the magazines and calendars of the time. Disney characters were prevalent, as well as the comic strips such as Al Capp's "L'il Abner," or Milton Caniff's "Terry and the Pirates." But the most widely copied artist was Alberto Vargas.

B-17 Waist gunner in action. *NASM*

Vargas was the premier pin-up artist of our time. Everyone has seen his work, whether it was a pin-up, a movie poster or a perfume ad. During the war, Vargas was the main artist for *Esquire* magazine, producing most of the artwork for the magazine's pin-up page and calendars. I think it would be safe to say that the arrival of a new *Esquire* with one of Vargas' exquisite airbrushed artworks was a red-letter day around the world.

The artwork could be painted on the plane by anyone. Those units fortunate enough to have talented artists produced excellent nose art. Some units went so far as to recruit artists, while some did without. It all had to do with the place, the people and the situation. Some of the remote outfits did not have the paint to do detailed work, while others had all they could ask for. So nose art came in all different shapes and sizes. The small ones could fit on a card table, while some of the B-29 artwork was bigger than a billboard.

There is no question that the golden age of nose art was during World War II and Korea. World War II was a time during which almost anything was allowed in an effort to boost morale and unit efficiency. But, as is the case with most things, a free hand led to some excesses and some censorship is evident in some of the artwork. After Korea, nose art all but disappeared from US aircraft. Artwork reappeared on a few Vietnam-vintage planes, but then it disappeared again. I am happy to report that nose art is making a comeback, slowly but surely, as commanders begin to see the positive effects that it has on air crews and their support personnel. Nose art can be beautiful, inspiring and in good taste.

—Sgt. Arnold Thurm

Cartoon from "Yank"—How nose art is really painted. . .

CAF collection

The Confederate Air Force in Harlingen, Texas, has perhaps the largest collection of authentic World War II nose art in the world. These are all panels that were cut off of aircraft being scrapped at Walnut Ridge, Arkansas, in 1946.

Although there is more than one version of this story, the most accurate one seems to be as follows: After the war, Brown and Root had a salvage operation at Walnut Ridge, where they scrapped out salvage aircraft for the aluminum under the name of Aircraft Conversion Company. The overall operation was so large, that at one time after World War II they owned more combat aircraft than the US government. This would have made them the first or second largest air force in the world.

Minot Pratt, general manager of the company, took a fancy to the nose art panels, and had a workman remove the "interesting" nose art with a fire axe. It seems that his idea was to build a fence around his property out of nose art. This never came to pass, so the panels were stored in the barn, and were later moved to west Texas when Pratt started a cattle company. The panels were given to the CAF in the mid-1960s. Regardless of the whys and wherefores, we are all in debt to this man for saving a piece of history. I would rather have the panels to look at than to fry eggs in.

Caption key
The following example will help you decipher the system I have used to identify each photograph.

Night Mission B-24-D 44-40891 234 BS 567 BG 47 AF Lost April 16, 1944. CAF/G. *Valant*

Night Mission is the nose art name
B-24-D is the aircraft type
44-40891 is the aircraft serial number
234 BS 567 BG 47 AF is the unit assignment
Lost April 16, 1944. is additional information about the aircraft
CAF/G. *Valant* is the source of the photograph for artifact/photographer

Source key
AFM stands for US Air Force Museum, Dayton, Ohio
NASM stands for National Air and Space Museum, Washington, DC
CAF stands for Confederate Air Force, Harlingen, Texas

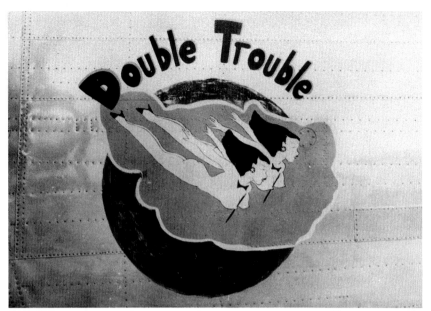

Double Trouble as first painted. Two props. *H. Russell*

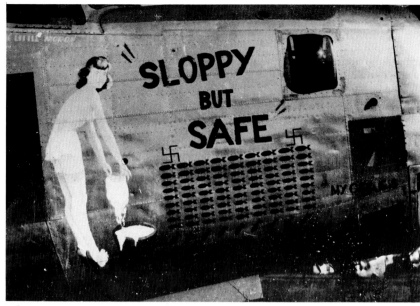

Sloppy But Safe on R&R AFM

Easy Maid stands on Iwo Jima, August 1945. *John Gardner*

Surprise Attack AFM

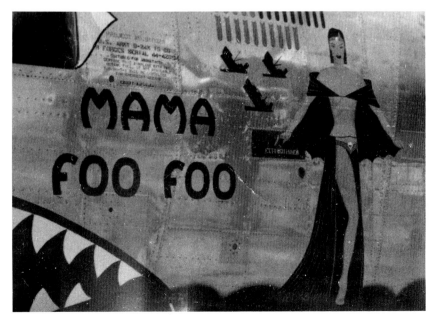

Mama Foo Foo *Clarence Ligocki*

Nobby's Harriet J B-17 The last photo of this aircraft before being scrapped at Walnut Ridge, AR, in 1946. *J. Wisler*

Brinkman nose art

Before the war, Mr. Brinkman was an advertising artist in the Chicago and St. Louis area. By the time he was drafted into the Army Air Corps he had six years experience as a commercial artist. There were no openings in special services for his talents, so he was assigned to a Guard unit at Davis-Monthan Army Air Base, Tucson, Arizona. Along with his other duties, he began to do art work and mess hall murals in the base area.

At this time of the war, November 1943, the 486th Bomb Group had just moved to Davis-Monthan for training. When the commander of the 834th Bomb Squadron, Capt W. D. Howell, saw some of Brinkman's work, he offered Brinkman a chance to transfer to the 834th. There and then, a nose art idea was born. Why not decorate each of

the twelve B-24s in the 834th with a sign of the Zodiac?

Early in April 1944, the 486th arrived at station 174, Sudbury, Suffolk, England, and Brinkman began painting the nose art on the B-24s. In total, Brinkman painted twelve Zodiacs, but you will find two Leos and no Taurus. In Brinkman's own words, "As I recall, the missing Zodiac was Taurus the Bull. All I remember was I started this sign three times and on the different B-24s, then they would take off and never return." As there are no records of any B-24 aircraft losses in the 834th, we can assume that the aircraft were transferred to other units.

The following photos are of Brinkman's sketches and finished work.

Brinkman sketch of **Leo** on B-24 41-29605 486 BG 834 BS 8 AF *Clarence Simonsen*

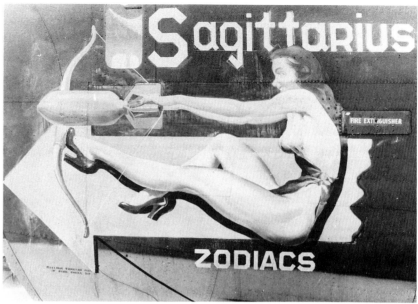

Sagittarius B-24 41-29400 486 BG 834 BS 8 AF Brinkman artwork. *AFM*

Brinkman's sketch of **American Beauty.** *C. Simonsen*

Brinkman sketch of **Aries.** *C. Simonsen*

Brinkman's sketch of **Silver Doller.** Note the pun **Doll-er** *C. Simonsen*

Hard To Get B-24 Brinkman nose art. *C. Simonsen*

Capricorn B-24 42-52744 486 BG 834 BS 8 AF Brinkman artwork. *C. Simonsen*

Brinkman sketch of **Taurus.** *C. Simonsen*

Brinkman's sketch of **Capricorn.** *C. Simonsen*

Aquaria B-24 42-52545 486 BG 834 BS 8 AF Brinkman artwork. *C. Simonsen*

Varga Girls

The following photographs are of some of the artwork of Alberto Vargas, which appeared in *Esquire* magazine during World War II. Interestingly, during this period Vargas painted under the name Varga—hence the name of this group of paintings, Varga Girls. *Esquire* holds the copyright on this artwork: Varga Girls copyright © (years of original publication) 1987 Esquire Assoc. Note the attempt to faithfully reproduce the drawing as closely as possible in most cases.

Vargas artwork. *Esquire.*

Vargas artwork. *Esquire.*

Vargas artwork. *Esquire.*

Vargas artwork. *Esquire.*

Hell's Angel B-17 42-97265 381BG 8AF Began service May 5, 1944; survived the war. *Esquire.* NASM

Hoosier Hot Shot B-17 42-38006 91BG 8AF Began service January 8, 1944; lost to Kassel April 19, 1944. *Esquire.* NASM

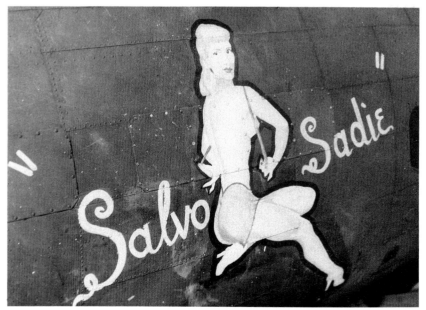

Salvo Sadie B-17 401BG AF *Esquire.* NASM

Sleepy Time Gal B-17 42-107112 Began service April 6, 1944; salvaged March 30, 1945. *Esquire. NASM*

Salvo Sadie B-17 401 BG 8 AF Jacket back. *Esquire. AFM*

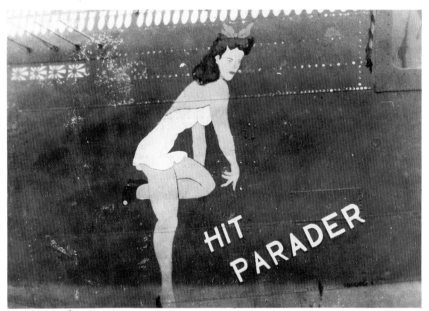

Hit Parader B-24 *Esquire. AFM*

Miss Fit B-24 *Esquire. AFM*

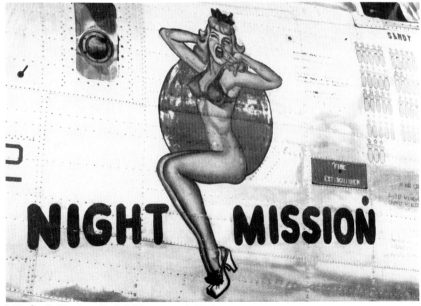

Night Mission B-24 *Esquire. AFM*

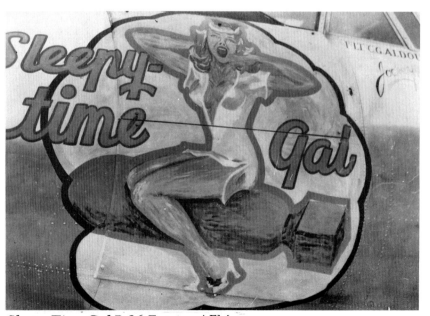

Sleepy Time Gal B-26 *Esquire. AFM*

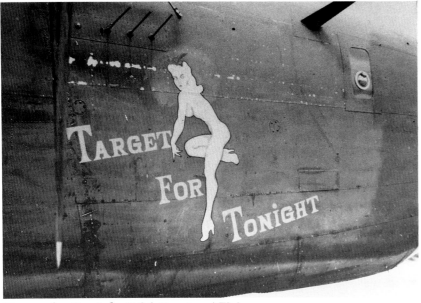

Target for Tonight B-24 *Esquire.* AFM

B-24 *Esquire.*

Mission Belle B-24-D 42-40389 400 BS Aircraft lost over Rabul November 18, 1943. *Esquire.* AFM

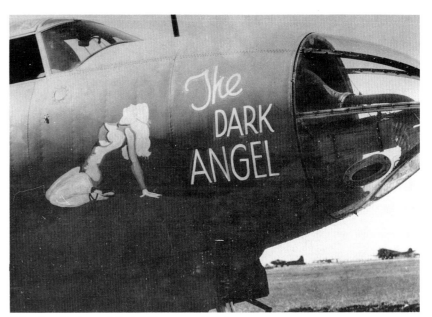

The Dark Angel B-26 *Esquire.* AFM

Scrumptious B-26 *Esquire.* AFM

"Over Exposed" *Esquire.* AFM

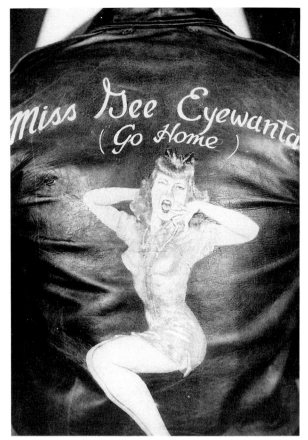

Miss Gee Eyewanta (Go Home) B-17 401
BG 8 AF *Esquire.* NASM

Other pin-ups were frequently used over
and over throughout the world. The following
was one of the more popular.

Wheel n Deal B-29 *Esquire.* AFM

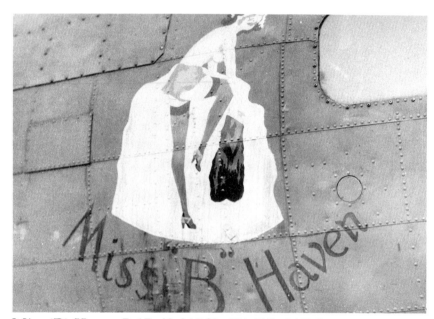

Miss 'B' Haven B-17 42-31863 401 BG 8AF Began service
February 6, 1944; salvaged February 19, 1945. *Esquire.* NASM

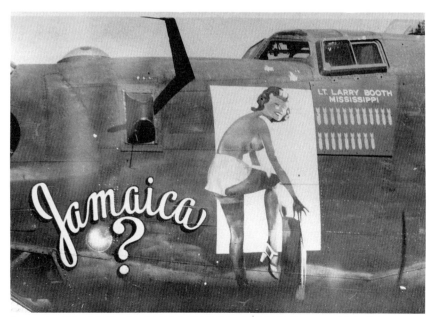

Jamaica? B-24-H 41-28746 785 BS 466 BG *Esquire.* NASM

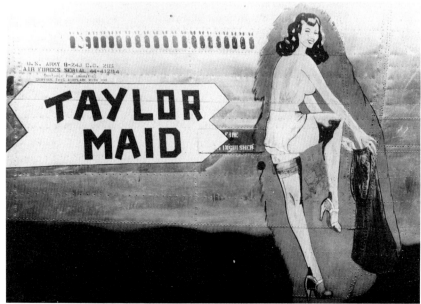

Taylor Maid B-24-J 44-41204 308 BG *Esquire.* AFM

:Our Gal: B-24 *Esquire. NASM*

Miss B Haven B-17 401 BG 8 AF *Esquire. NASM*

B-26 42-107625 *Esquire. AFM*

Little Pink Panties B-26-C 42-107841 *Esquire. AFM*

Vargas artwork. *Esquire.*

5 Grand B-17 43-37716 96 8 AF AFM

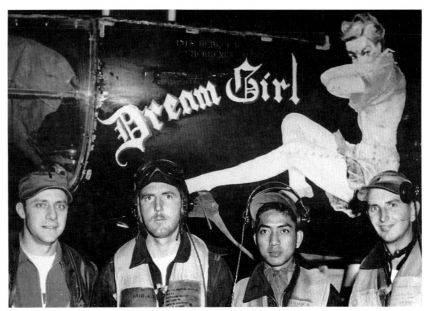

Dream Girl in service in Korea. NASM

Lucky Strike B-24 NASM

A Bit o' Lace C. Simonsen

The original sketch by Caniff for *A Bit o' Lace.* C. Simonsen

The cartoon with Miss Lace as seen in the army camp newspapers. C. Simonsen

The Shack C. Simonsen

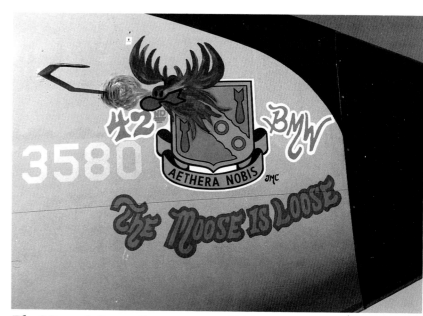

The Moose is Loose Contemporary USAF nose art. J. Adderly

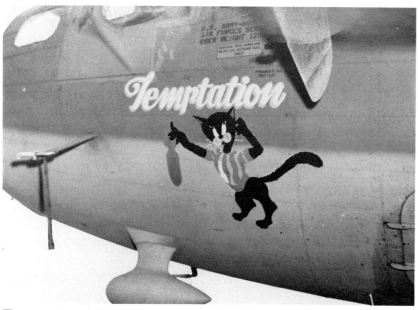

Temptation B-17 42-30188 96 BG 8AF Salvaged Feburary 4, 1944. AFM

Old Irongut B-17 NASM

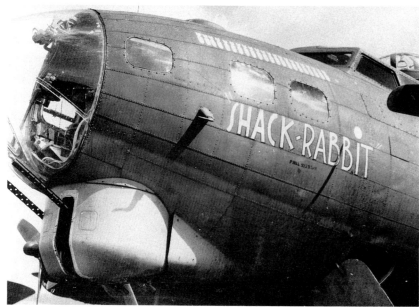

Shack Rabbit B-17 42-3318 96 BG 8 AF Lost on a mission to Kerlin/Bastard on September 23, 1945. NASM

Sugar Puss B-17 42-3088 94 BG 8 AF AFM

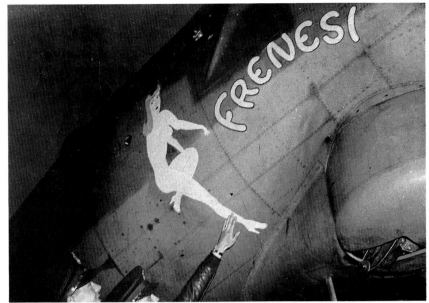

Frenesi B-17 Pronounced "Free n Easy," this 8th AF B-17 piloted by Lt. Cely is shown after a large raid—"just a series of holes held together by some metal"—with three wounded gunners. *AFM*

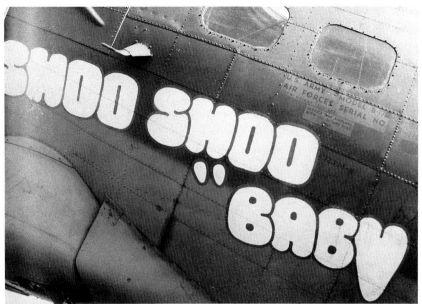

Shoo Shoo Baby B-17 42-31669 303BG 8 AF Lost April 24, 1944, over Landsberg. *NASM*

Patches n' Prayers B-17 42-37733 381 BG 8 AF Began service February 22, 1944; Lost April 18, 1944. *NASM*

Mary Cary B-17 42-97405 360 BS 303BG 8AF Began service April 30, 1944; lost June 22, 1944. *NASM*

Sunkist Special B-17 91 BG 8AF *Andrews AFB*

Oops—what happened to the "Kist?" *NASM*

Jacket patch and map from the China-Burma-India (CBI) Theater.

Miss Bea Havin B-17 NASM

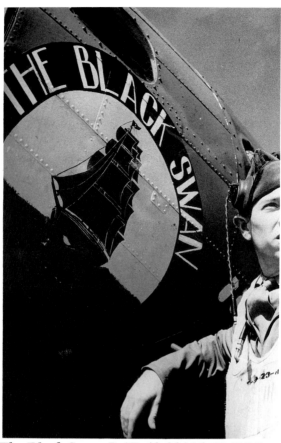

The Black Swan B-17 42-29895 324BSQ 91BG 8AF NASM

Scrappy Jr B17 44-83264 452 BG 8AF NASM

Screwball Express B-17 42-97128 379BG 8AF Began service March 23, 1944; lost April 5, 1945. NASM

Yankee Belle B-17-G 42-32085 91 BG 8AF Began service July 10, 1944; Lost on a mission to Berlin February 3, 1945. NASM

Lightning Strikes B-17 42-3073 563BS 388BG 8AF NASM

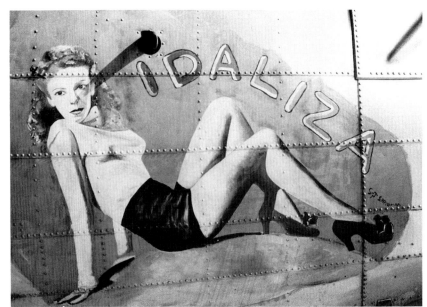

Idaliza B-17 42-97546 303BG 8AF Began service March 12, 1944; declared beyond repair January 30, 1945. *NASM*

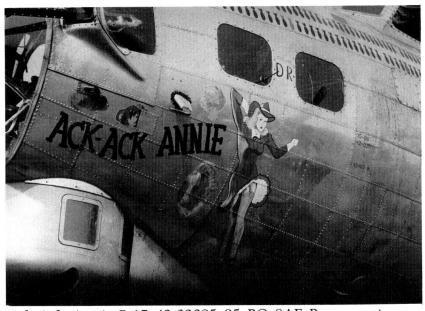

Ack-Ack Annie B-17 42-32095 95 BG 8AF Began service March 16, 1944; survived the war. *NASM*

Alley-Oop B-17 42-5854 303BG 8AF Began service with 303DR on July 13, 1943, returned to US April 15, 1944. *NASM*

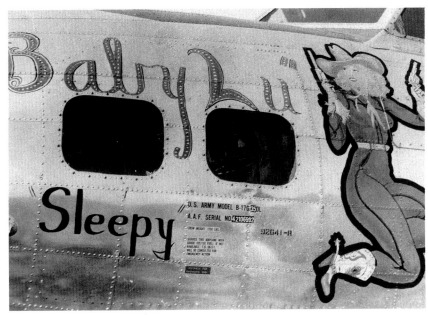

Baby Lu B-17 42-106992 401 BG 8AF NASM

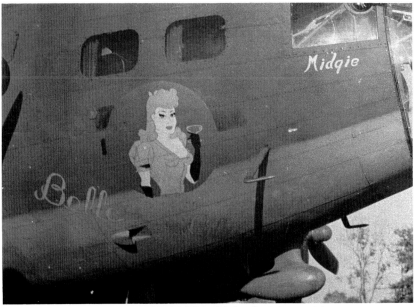

Belle of the Blue B-17 42-30094 385 BG 8AF NASM

Black Swan B-17 42-29895 91B6 8AF Began service May 23, 1943; lost December 31, 1943, on a mission to Bordeaux the day after a mid-air collision with ***Duke of Paducah.*** *NASM*

Blooming Grove B-17 92 BG 8AF *NASM*

Blue Dreams B-17 42-37761 323BS 91BG 8AF Began service January 4, 1943; salvaged March 7, 1944. *NASM*

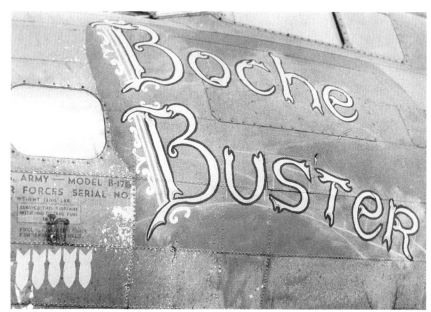

Boche Buster B-17 42-31087 401 BG 8AF Began service November 8, 1943; lost over Germany October 7, 1944. *NASM*

Bundles for Berlin B-17 92BG 8AF *NASM*

Bunky B-17 42-31542 91 BG 8AF Began service March 12, 1944; lost July 19, 1944. *NASM*

Can Do B-17 305 BG 8AF NASM

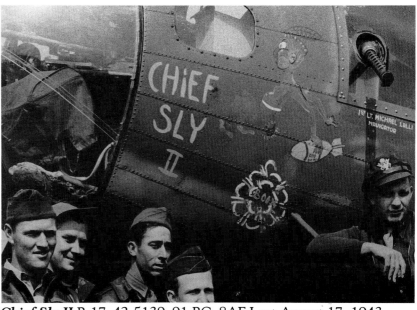

Chief Sly II B-17 42-5139 91 BG 8AF Lost August 17, 1943, on a mission to Schweinfurt. *NASM*

Chow Hound B-17 42-31367 91 BG 8AF Began service January 25, 1944; lost August 8, 1944. *NASM*

The Bat Outa Hell B-17 41-9154 92 BG 8AF Salvaged June 26, 1944. *AFM*

!!Classy Chassy!! B-17 42-31137 388BG Interned in Sweden after a forced landing April 9, 1944. *NASM*

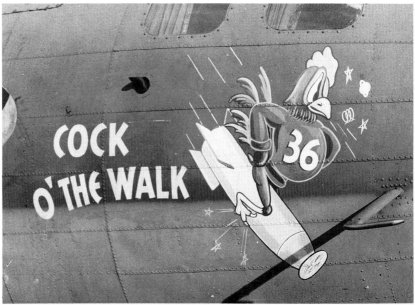

Cock o' the Walk B-17 42-30800 388BG 8AF Lost February 29, 1944, at Brunswick. *NASM*

Colonel Bub B-17 381BG NASM

Daddy's Delight B-17-G 42-97422 303BG 8AF Began service June 2, 1944; salvaged April 7, 1945. NASM

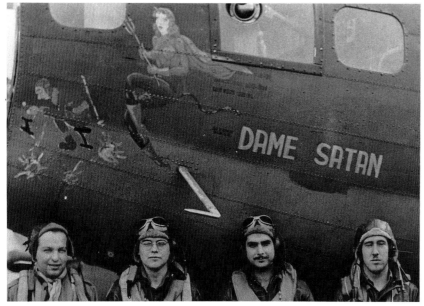

Dame Satan B-17 322BS 91BG 8AF Lost on a mission to Schweinfurt, August 17, 1943. NASM

Dame Satan II B-17 42-31070 322BS 91BG 8AF Returned to the US June 18, 1944. NASM

Delta Rebel B-17 91BG 322BS 8AF AFM

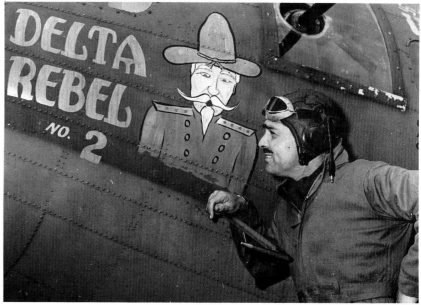

Delta Rebel No2 B-17 42-5077 Clark Gable, a B-17 waist gunner in the 8AF admires *Delta Rebel No2* 91BG 322BS 8AF lost August 12, 1942, on a mission to Gelsenkirchen. AFM

Demo Darling B-17 42-39774 323BS 91BG 8AF NASM

Desperate Journey B-17 42-3053 Maj. Aycock stands beside B-17 at the 324BS 91BG 8AF. NASM

Dog Breath B-17-G 42-31330 401BG NASM

Better Do'er! B-17 44-6977 303BG 8AF Began service February 1, 1945; survived the war. NASM

Doris-Jr B-17 NASM

Dottie B-17 92BG 8AF NASM

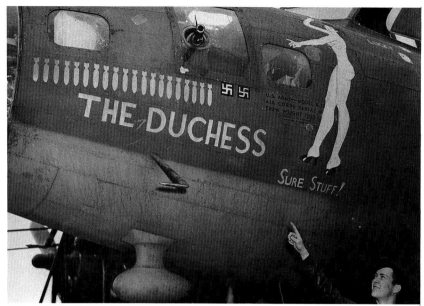

The Duchess (Sure Stuff)! B-17 8AF NASM

Duke of Paducah B-17 401BS 91BG 8AF The bent nose is from a mid-air collision with **Black Swan.** AFM

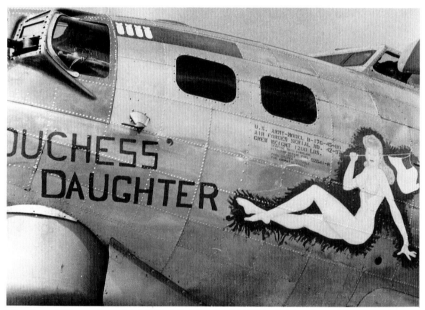

Duchess' Daughter B-17G-45-80 42-97272 303BG 8AF Joined the 303 on April 19, 1944. NASM

Wreck of **Duchess' Daughter** after wheels-up landing July 1944. Note all four engines were off before landing. NASM

Dynamite John B-17 401BG 8AF NASM

Eager Beaver B-17 793BS India. NASM

The Eagle's Wrath B-17 91BG Lost August 17, 1943, on a mission to Schweinfurt. *NASM*

El Lobo B-17 42-24593 305 BG 8AF Lost February 4, 1943, over Emdem. Flash suppressors on 50-cal. machine guns. *NASM*

Equipoise B-17 42-30580 92BG *NASM*

E-Rat-Icator B-17G-10-VE 42-38970 452BG 8AF Note flack hole repair panels. Bomb is labeled "rat poison." *NASM*

Exterminator B-17 92BG 8AF *NASM*

Extra Special B-17 322BS 91BG 8AF *NASM*

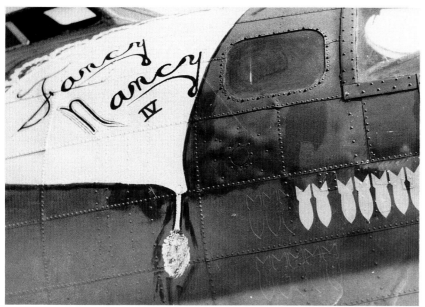

Fancy Nancy IV B-17 42-31662 401BG 8AF Salvaged April 25, 1945. *NASM*

FDR's Potato Peeler Kids B-17 42-5243 303BG *NASM*

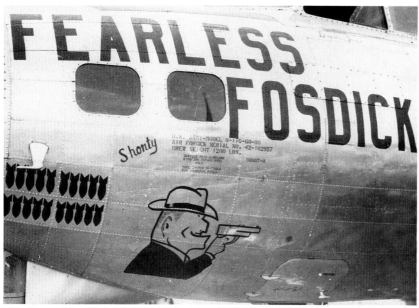

Fearless Fosdick B-17G-GQ-BO #42-102957 358BS 303BG 8AF *NASM*

Fickle Finger of Fate B-17 42-3335 385 BG 8AF Salvaged April 9, 1945. *NASM*

Flak Eater B-17 44-6009 305BG 8AF Began service April 17, 1944; survived the war. *NASM*

Flak Flirter B-17G 43-38366 493 BG 8AF Salvaged April 15, 1945 *NASM*

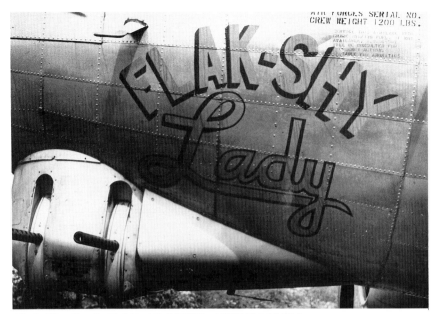

Flak-Shy Lady B-17 43-39326 452BG NASM

Flyin' Hobo B-17 381BG NASM

Flying Jenny B-17 525BS 379BG 8AF NASM

Forget Me Not II B-17 381BG 8AF NASM

Fort Alamo II B-17F-B5-HO #42-29896 Italy. NASM

Fort Worth Gal B-17G-40-DL 44-6095 381BG NASM

The Fox B-17G-05-BO 43-37657 381 BG 8AF Began service
June 10, 1944; salvaged February 14, 1945. NASM

French Dressing B-17 381 BG 8AF NASM

Geezil B-17 42-5404 306 BG 8AF Began service February 25,
1943; lost October 30, 1944. NASM

Green Mountain Rambler B-17 303BG 8AF NASM

Gremlin's Delite B-17 42-3120 381BG NASM

Gremlin Gus II B-17 42-30595 388BG 8AF NASM

Gremlin Trainer B-17 305BGP NASM

Happy Bottom B-17G 42-102664 Edward G. Robinson christens the B-17 381BG 8AF. NASM

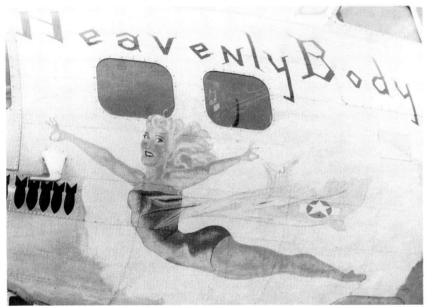

Heavenly Body B-17 42-37812 390BG Lost March 8, 1944, on a mission to Berlin. NASM

Heinie Headhunters B-17 NASM

Hell's Angel B-17C-45-CO #42-97265 401BG 8AF NASM

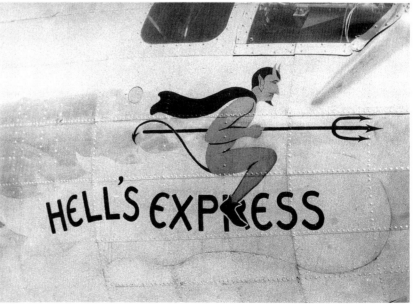

Hell's Express B-17 401BG 8AF NASM

Hell's Halo B-17 322BS 91BG 8AF NASM

Hell Zapoppin B-17 92BG 8AF NASM

Henn's Revenge B-17 44-8427 303BG 8 AF Began service October 23, 1943; declared beyond repair April 10, 1945. NASM

Hey Daddy B-1743-8036 91BG 8AF NASM

Hi-Doc! B-17 NASM

Hit Parade Jr B-17 385 BG 8AF NASM

Holy Mackeral! B-17 41-42609 303BG 8AF Began service
October 24, 1942; lost over Paris April 4, 1943. *NASM*

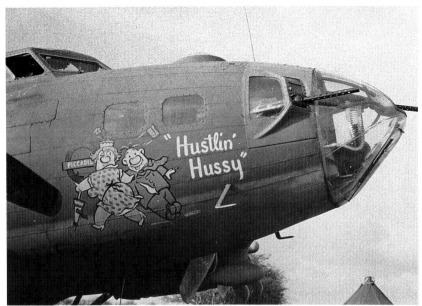

Hustlin' Hussy B-17 42-30354 385 BG 8AF Lost on a mission
to Frankfurt January 29, 1944. *Andrews AFB*

Incendiary Blonde B-17 44-6951 91 BG 8AF Began service
November 4, 1944; survived the war. *NASM*

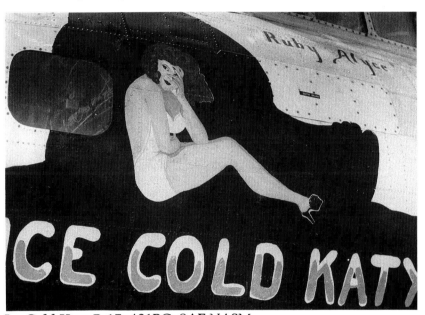

Ice Cold Katy B-17 401BG 8AF *NASM*

Ice Col' Katy B-17 381 BG 8AF *NASM*

Jack the Ripper B-17 41-24490 324BS 91BG Lost February 22,
1944. *NASM*

Jap-Happy B-17E #41-2520 NASM

Jezebel B-17 91BG 8AF NASM

The Joker B-17F 42-29888 NASM

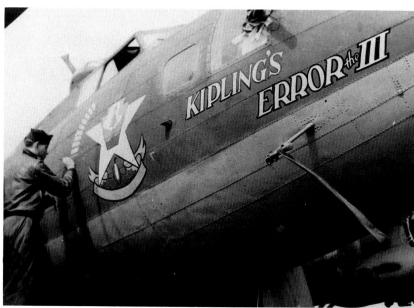

Kipling's Error the III B-17 42-5885 96BG 8AF Lost on a mission to Rostock April 11, 1944. NASM

The Klap-Trap II 42-30130 96BG 8AF Lost over Ludwigshafen, January 7, 1944. B-17

Knock-Out Dropper B-17 41-24605 359BS 303BG 8AF NASM

Lady Satan B-17 42-97175 452 BG 8AF Lost February 6, 1945. NASM

Lewd Angel B-17G-95-BO 43-38755 91BG 8AF NASM

Liberty Belle B-17F 42-30096 544BS 385 BG 8AF NASM

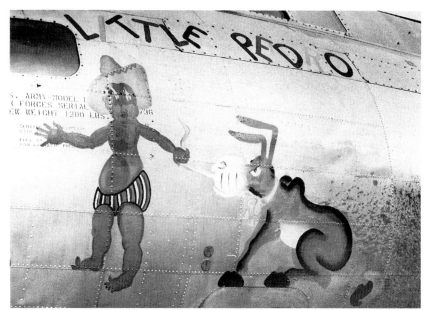

Little Pedro B-17 43-37736 401BG 8AF Began service June 10, 1944; salvaged November 8, 1944. NASM

Little Tush B-17 42-102595 303BS 8AF Began service June 6, 1944 (D-Day); salvaged August 8, 1944. NASM

Los Lobos B-17 NASM

Madame Shoo Shoo B-17G 43-37707 322BS 91BG 8AF Began service June 28, 1944; beyond repair April 8, 1945. *NASM*

Madame Queen B-17 42-97931 401BG 8AF Began service June 1, 1944; survived the war. *NASM*

Margie Mae B-17 42-5847 381BG 8AF Lost on a mission to Gelsenkirchen August 12, 1943. *NASM*

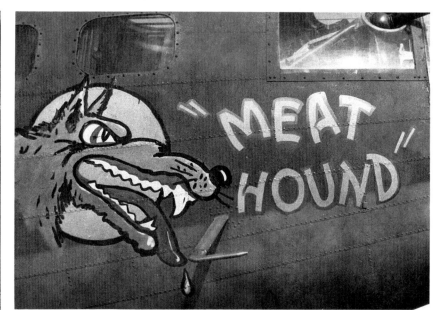

Meat Hound B-17 42-29524 303 BG 8AF Began service July 30, 1943; lost over Oschersleben January 11, 1944. *NASM*

Mis-Abortion B-17 381BG This name offended someone, and was later changed to "Stuff." *NASM*

Stuff B-17 42-2371 *NASM*

Miss Umbriago B-1742-97187 360 BS 303BG 8AF Began service March 26, 1944; lost on a mission to Magdeburg, September 28, 1944. *NASM*

Mollita B-17 43-37817 452 BG 8AF Salvaged July 14, 1944. *NASM*

The Mustang (Buck Shot) B-17F *NASM*

Miss Dee-Day B-17 8AF 305BF Could mean Miss D-Day (invasion) or misty day—common in England. *NASM*

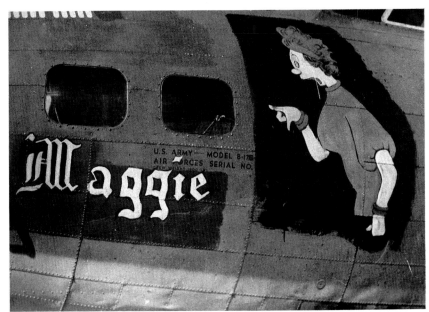

Maggie B-17 42-31091 401BG 8AF Began service November 11, 1943; lost September 11, 1944. *NASM*

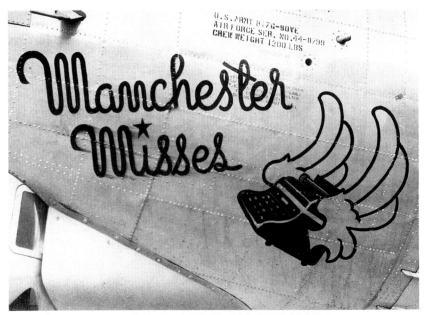

Manchester Misses B-17G 452BG #44-8799 *NASM*

Margie B-17 43-38379 323BS 91BG 8AF NASM

Mary Lou B-17 42-97504 323BS 91BG 8AF Salvaged October 14, 1944. NASM

Minnie the Mermaid B-17 42-31614 381BG 8AF Began service January 21, 1944; lost February 22, 1944. NASM

Miss Lace B-17 42-102411 303BG 8AF Began service April 30, 1944; salvaged March 28, 1945. NASM

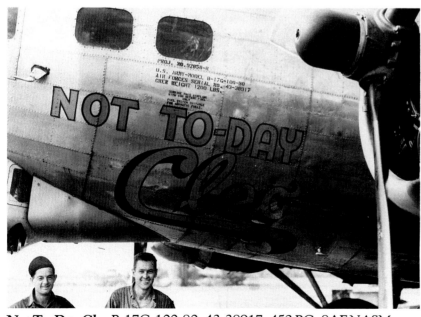

Not To-Day Cleo B-17G-100-80 43-38917 452 BG 8AF NASM

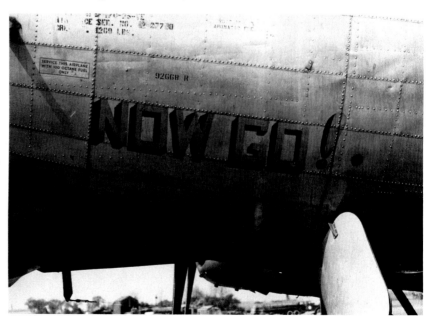

Now Go! B-17 42-97780 452BG 8AF Began service April 28, 1944; survived the war. NASM

Old Bill B-17 42-29673 8AF Began service April 6, 1943; salvaged April 16, 1943. NASM

Ol' Mac B-17 305BG 8AF NASM

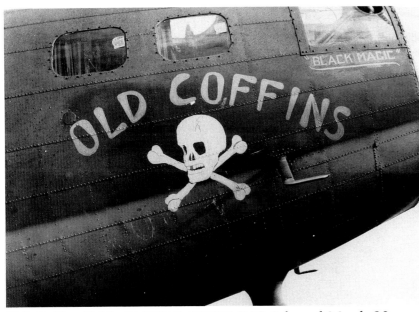

Old Coffins B-17 42-30018 381BG 8AF Salvaged March 20, 1944. NASM

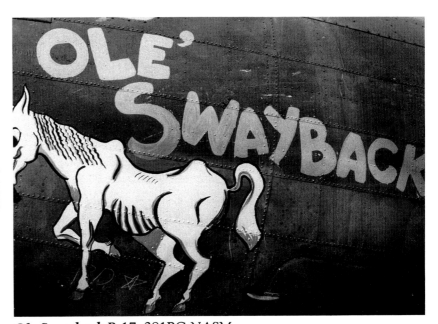

Ole Swayback B-17 381BG NASM

Oh Happy Day B-17C-95-BO 43-38790 NASM

Ooold Soljer B-17 41-24559 303BG 360BS 8AF Began service October 24, 1942; salvaged April 1, 1943. NASM

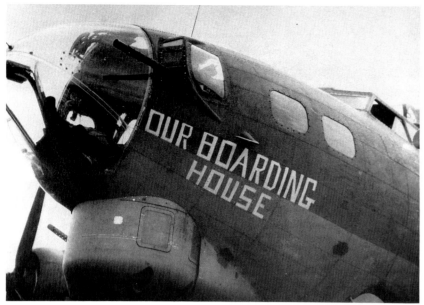

Our Boarding House B-17 381BG NASM

Pakawalup B-17 42-97630 457BG 8AF NASM

Patty Jo B-17 42-31242 563BS 388BG 8AF NASM

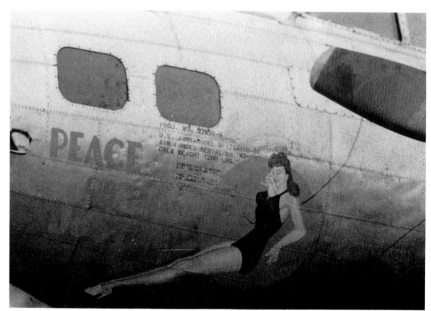

Peace or Bust B-17 91BG 8AF NASM

Pella Tulip B-17G 42-102703 381BG Began service April 22, 1944; salvaged October 14, 1944. NASM

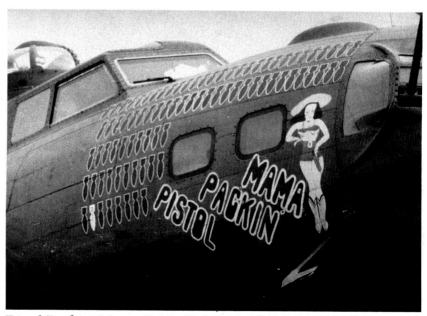

Pistol Packin' Mama B-17 42-30791 305BG 8AF NASM

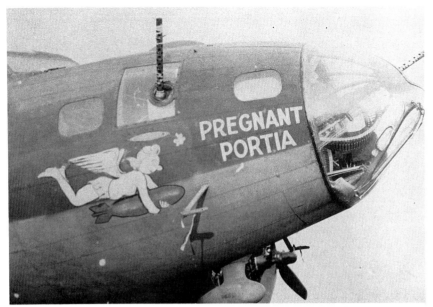

Pregnant Portia B-17 42-30263 385BG 8AF Salvaged November 2, 1943. *NASM*

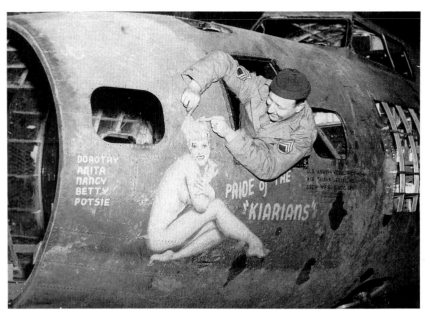

Pride of the "Kiarians" B-17 Undergoes major repairs. *NASM*

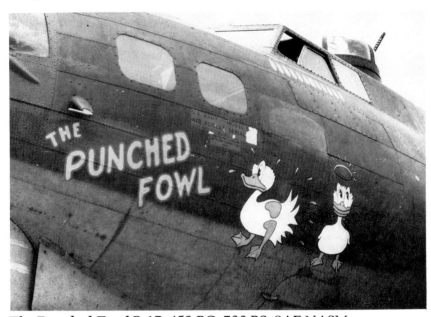

The Punched Fowl B-17 452 BG 730 BS 8AF *NASM*

Ramp Rooster B-17 42-107188 398BG 8AF Began service May 5, 1944; lost December 29, 1944. *NASM*

Rat poison Tail art on rear gunner area. B-17 *NASM*

Redmond Annie B-17 Annie is riding a mule and has a B-17 on a string. *NASM*

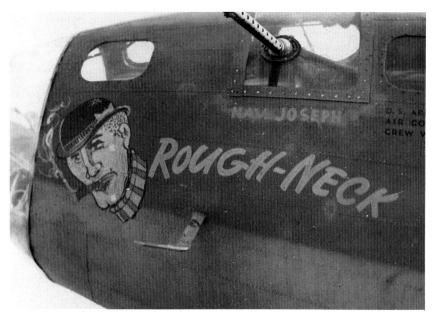

Rough-Neck B-17 North Africa. *NASM*

Roxy's Special B-17 43-38348 322BS 91BG 8AF Began service August 18, 1944; lost on a mission to Ludwigshafen September 8, 1944. *NASM*

Rusty Dusty B-17 44-6578 322BS 91BG 8AF Began service December 7, 1944; salvaged April 4, 1945. *NASM*

Sack Time B-17 42-102544 303BG 8AF Began service April 12, 1944; lost over Dresden April 17, 1945. *NASM*

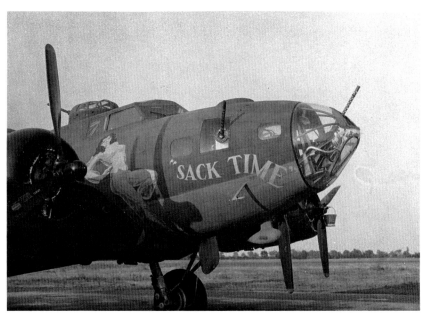

"Sack Time" B-17 42-5912 385 BG 8AF Lost to Regensburg August 17, 1943. Note bucket on prop spinner. *NASM*

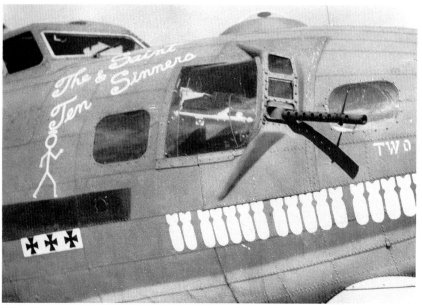

The Saint & Ten Sinners B-17 401BG *NASM*

Scorchy II B-17 42-97058 359BS 303BG 8AF Began March 27, 1944; lost over Aschaffenburg January 21, 1945. NASM

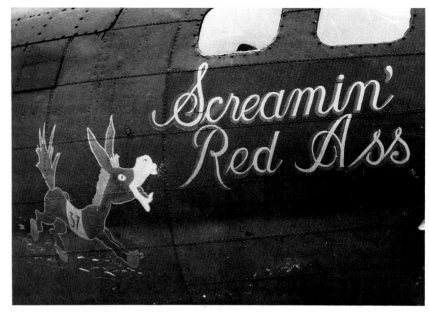

Screamin' Red Ass B-17 42-30340 388BG 563 BS 8AF Lost March 8, 1944, on a mission to Berlin. NASM

Screw B-17 NASM

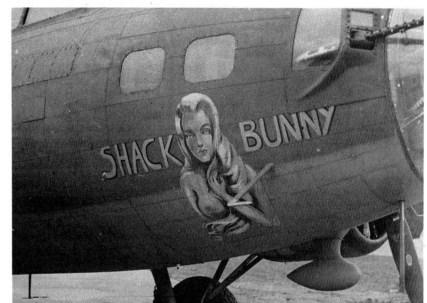

Shack Bunny B-17 42-5914 385 BG 8AF NASM

Shangi-La Lil B-17 42-29754 303BG 360BS 8AF Began service June 17, 1943; lost over Watten August 27, 1943. NASM

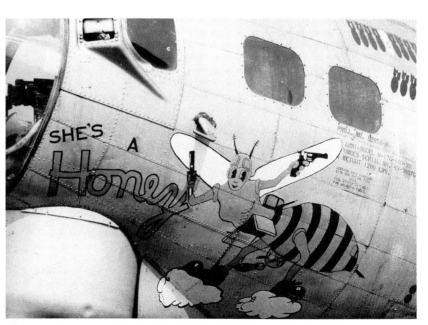

She's A Honey B-17-G 43-38970 305BG 8 AF NASM

49

Shoo Shoo Baby B-17 42-97311 303 BG 8AF Began service April 13, 1944; survived the war. *NASM*

Shoo-Shoo Baby B-24 *AFM*

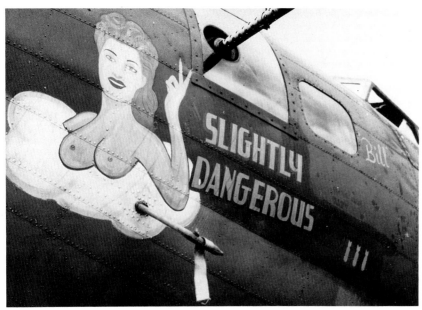

Slightly Dangerous B-17 42-3293 388 BG 563 BS 8 AF Lost to Stuttgart September 6, 1943, on nineteenth mission. Caught fire after a fighter attack; five crewman survived. *NASM*

Smashing Time B-17 43-38158 381BG 8 AF Salvaged January 21, 1945. *NASM*

Spare Parts B-17 305 BG 8 AF *NASM*

Sparky B-17 44-8125 360BS 303 BG 8 AF *NASM*

Special Delivery B-17-G 42-102496 359 BS 303 BG 8 AF
Began April 30, 1944; crashed September 18, 1944. *NASM*

Stag Party B-17-G 43-37837 305 BG 8 AF *NASM*

Star Dust B-17 43-38901 322 BS 91 BG 8AF *NASM*

Stars and Stripes B-17 42-3544 385 BG 8AF Lost January 5,
1944, on a mission to Bordeaux. *NASM*

Stinky B-17 322 BS 91 BG 8 AF *NASM*

Stric Nine B-17 42-29475 91 BG 323BS 8AF Began service
March 7, 1943; lost on a mission to Caen July 10, 1943. *NASM*

Swamp Fire B-17 42-32024 525 BS 379 BG 8 AF 100th mission marker. The aircraft survived the war. NASM

Sweet Dish B-17 44-6586 91 BG 8 AF NASM

Texas Chubby-The J'Ville Jolter B-17 42-31634 8 AF Lost August 16, 1944. NASM

Target for Tonite B-17 41-24615 305BG 8 AF NASM

Tempest Turner B-17 43-38216 493BG 8 AF NASM

Tiger Girl B-17 388BG 560BS 8 AF NASM

To Tokyo B-17 NASM

Toots B-17 42-29606 303BG 8AF Began service April 6, 1943; lost on a mission to Hamburg July 25, 1943. NASM

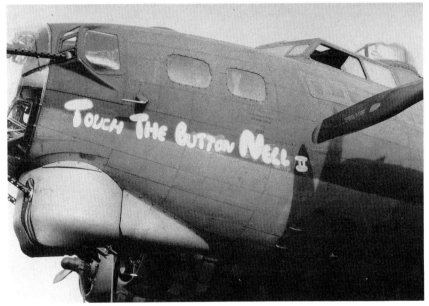

Touch the Button Nell II B-17 42-38117 381 BG 8AF Began service February 26, 1944; lost July 4, 1944. NASM

Tower of London B-17 91BG 8AF NASM

Turd Burd B-17 305 BG 8AF NASM

Twan-n-g-g-g B-17-G 42-97838 401BG 8 AF NASM

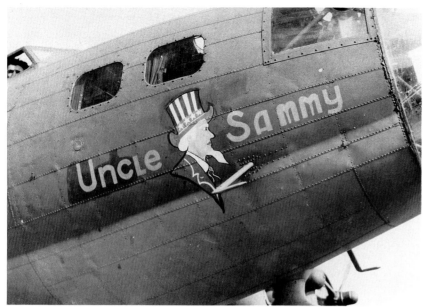

Uncle Sammy B-17 381 BG NASM

Under Ground Farmer B-17-G 44-6020 381 BG 8AF Began service April 28, 1944; lost October 10, 1944. NASM

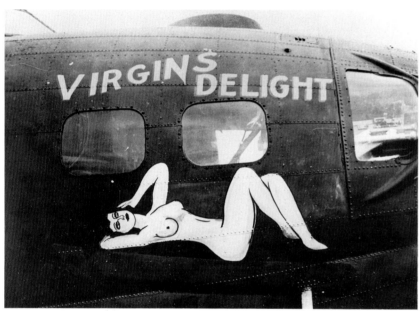

Virgins Delight B-17 42-3352 94 BG 8AF Lost on a mission to Solingen November 30, 1943. NASM

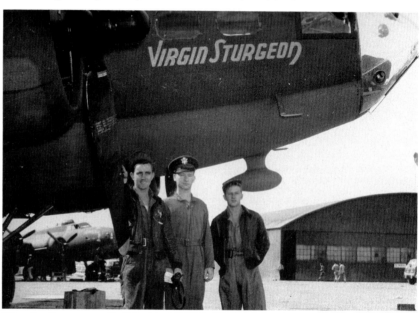

Virgin Sturgeon B-17 42-30334 390 BG 8 AF Lost on a mission to Frankfurt January 29, 1944. NASM

Hulcher's Vultures B-17 42-39845 388BG 8AF Lost April 28, 1944. NASM

Wallaroo B-17 42-3029 303 BG 8AF Began service April 9, 1943; lost on a mission to Pas De Calais January 14, 1944. NASM

Wee Willie B-17 42-31333 322 BS 91 BG 8 AF Began service December 20, 1943; lost April 8, 1945. NASM

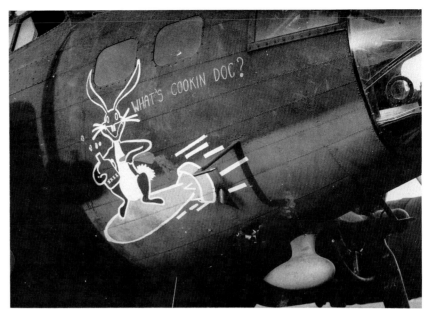

What's Cookin Doc? B-17 41-24525 384BG 8 AF Lost over Ludwigshafen January 7, 1944. NASM

Whirlaway B-17 381 BG NASM

Wicked Witch B-17 323 BS 91 BG 8 AF NASM

The Wild Hare B-17 42-31515 91BG 324BS 8 AF Began service January 21, 1944; lost on a mission to Bremen November 26, 1944. NASM

Wolfess B-17 42-29953 305 BG 8 AF Salvaged November 15, 1943. NASM

Woosh Woosh B-17 305 BG 8AF NASM

Yankee Doodle Dandy James Cagney christens a B-17 42-39953 of the 390 BG. Lost to Leipzig April 29, 1944. NASM

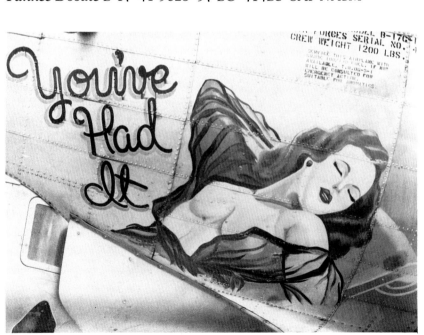

Yankee Doodle B-17 41-9023 97 BG 414BS 8AF NASM

Yankee Rebel B-17 381 BG 8AF NASM

You've Had It B-17 43-39143 452 BG 8AF NASM

You've Had It! B-17 NASM

Yankee Gal B-17 42-29557 384 BG 8AF Salvaged October 23, 1943. NASM

Yankee Gal B-17 43-37844 91 BG 8AF NASM

The Zoot Suiters B-17 42-30235 95BG 8AF NASM

Zootie Cutie B-17-G 43-37616 NASM

B-17 NASM

———*But Right* B-17 NASM

B-17 NASM

B-17 NASM

B-17 NASM

———**Pride** B-17 NASM

Anxious Angel B-17-G 91 BG 8 AF AFM

Bam Bam B-17 42-37893 Joined the 303 BG November 18, 1943. AFM

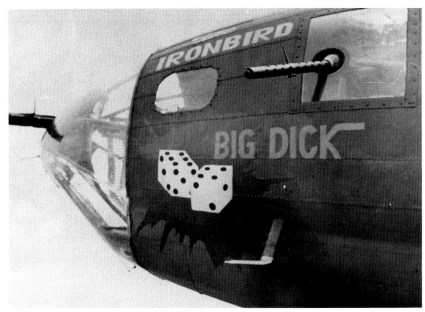

Better Duck B-17 43-8990 95 BG 8 AF Flew 53 missions prior to returning to the US in July 1945. Lt. Cook, looking from the window, was lost on May 7, 1945 (the day before V-E Day) on a chow hound mercy mission to northern Europe. It is believed that the plane was lost to small arms fire. The aircraft—B-17 44-8640—was the last 8 AF plane lost during the war. *Cook Collection*

Big Dick B-17 8 AF Named for the dice roll "Big Dick from Dixie." AFM

The Biggest Bird B-17 AFM

Bomb Boogie B-17 42-5763 401 BS 91 BG 8 AF Began March 9, 1943; lost to Stuttgart September 6, 1943. AFM

Bomber Dear B-17-C-45-BO 42-97234 91 BG 8 AF AFM

Cabin in the Sky B-17-F 42-30338 571 BS 390 BG 8 AF Major Brown looks out of the cabin February 25, 1945. AFM

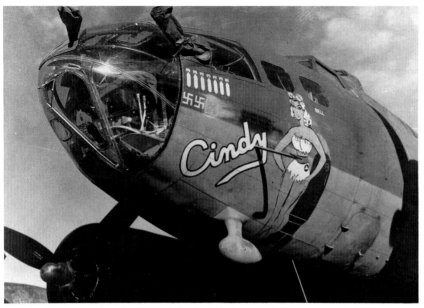

Cindy B-17 2-5821 379 BG 8 AF One of the original 379th aircraft. Lost to Gelsenkirchen August 12, 1943. *AFM*

Dear Mom B-17 *AFM*

Dry Martini & the Cocktail Kids (The 4th) B-17-F 364 BS 305 BG 8 AF Note two swans plus twenty fighter kills. *AFM*

Fearless Fosdick B-17-G 43-37890 401 BG 8 AF *AFM*

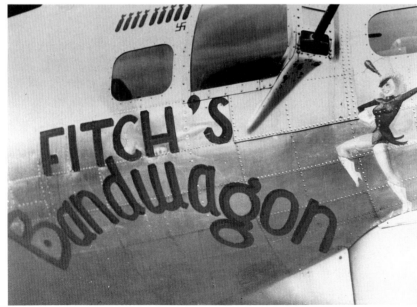

Fitch's Bandwagon B-17 42-107043 401 BG 8 AF Began March 23, 1944; beyond repair after crash two weeks later. *AFM*

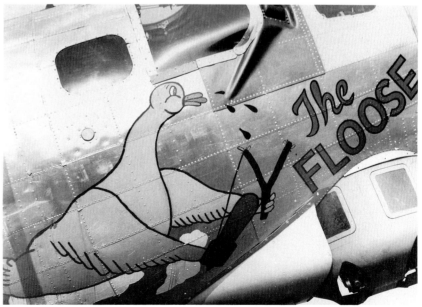

The Floose B-17 42-97298 358 BS 303 BG 8 AF Had over 100 missions when it was destroyed in a wheels-up landing. *AFM*

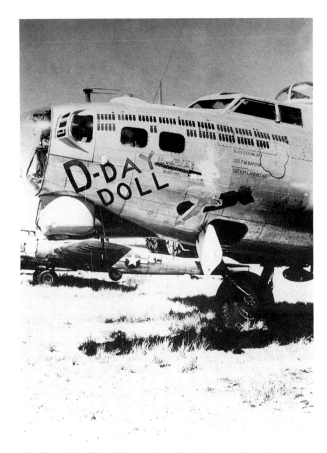

D Day Doll B-17 447 BG 8 AF In the Arizona desert waiting to be sold for scrap. *AFM*

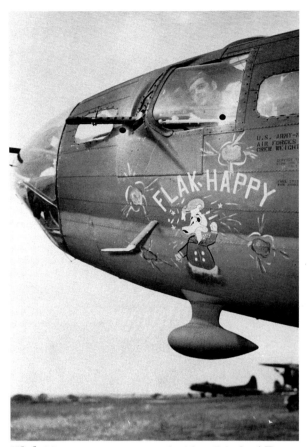

Flak-Happy B-17 92 BG 327 BS 8 AF *AFM*

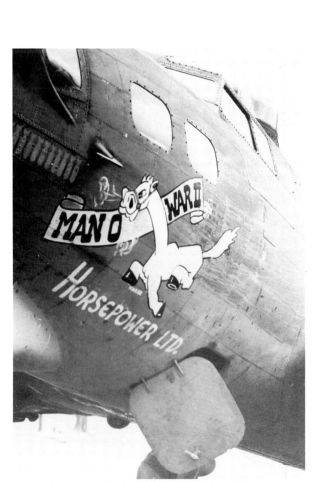

Man O War II B-17 42-38083 91 BG 8 AF Named after the famous race horse. It joined the 91st January 10, 1944; failed to return from a mission to Merseburg November 2, 1944. *AFM*

Sheriff's Posse B-17 42-97151 91 BG 8 AF 1st Lt. Robert E. Sheriff of Cleveland, OH, polishes the star on his aircraft's nose art. Joined the 91st March 3, 1944; declared beyond repair after a crash landing March 23, 1944. *AFM*

61

Goonie B-17 11BG 98 BS Named for the Goonie Bird, which had a semi-crash landing style. *AFM*

Hikin' for Home B-17 42-107027 91 BG 8 AF 73 Joined April 7, 1944, named "Anne." *AFM*

Impatient Virgin B-17 42-3273 95 BG 8 AF The nose art seems to express the mood of the aircraft after a nose-down landing December 24, 1943. *University of Texas at Dallas Collection.*

Grim Reaper B-17 97 BG North Africa. The Grim Reaper had flown 35 missions when this photo was taken. 7 crew members have purple hearts and have shot down 10 aircraft, 6 on one mission. Over Trapani, Sicily, 3 gunners were wounded, one engine lost, and a fire broke out in the bomb bay area. *AFM*

Holy Terror III B-17 100 BG 8 AF *AFM*

Impatient Virgin B-17-F 306 BG *AFM*

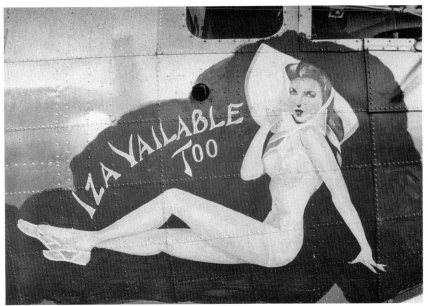

Iza Vailable Too B-17 42-97254 360 BS 303 BG 8 AF AFM

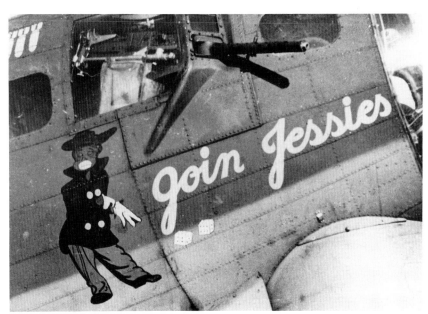

Goin Jessies B-17 42-31051 100 BG 8 AF Lost March 6, 1944,

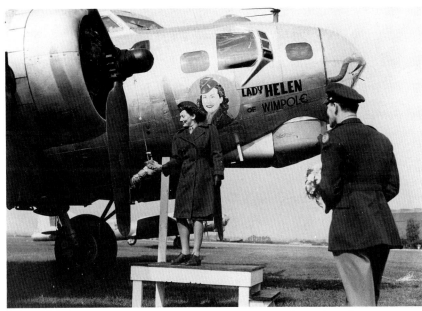

Lady Helen of Wimpole B-17 91 BG 8AF Lady Helen christens her. B-17. AFM

Lakanuki B-17 42-4176 379 BG 8 AF Interned in Sweden January 5, 1944. AFM

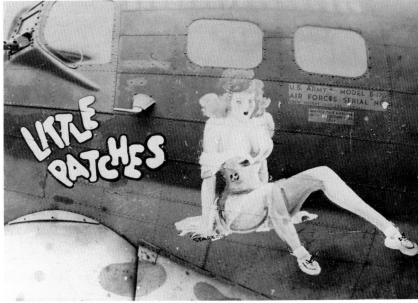

Little Patches B-17 42-31578 401 BS 91 BG 8 AF Joined the 91st December 29, 1943; lost March 6, 1944, on a mission to Berlin. AFM

The Lucky Strike B-17 41-29923 381 BG 8 AF Began service September 11, 1943; salvaged January 5, 1944. AFM

Madame-X B-17 11 BG 98 BS Photo taken on Guadalcanal. AFM

Maximum Effort B-17 43-38267 401 BG 8 AF Joined the 401st August 25, 1944, declared beyond repair November 30, 1944. NASM

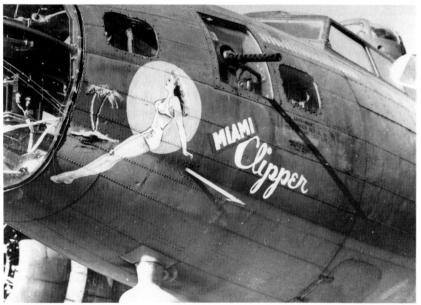

Miami Clipper B-17 42-29815 91 BG 8 AF AFM

Miss Slip Stream B-17 43-38202 91 BG 8 AF Began August 8, 1944; lost to Merseburg November 2, 1944. AFM

Miss Ouachita B-17 42-3040 91 BG 8 AF This aircraft served with the 303 and 306 BG prior to joining the 91st August 22, 1943. It was shot down by Luftwaffe pilot Maj. Heinz Bar February 21, 1944 over Gutersloh. AFM

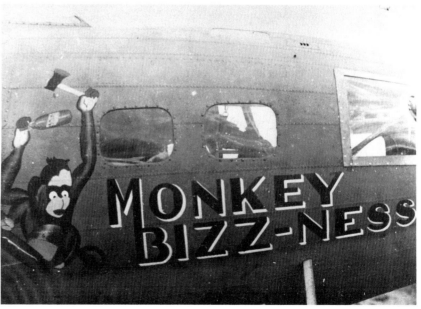

Monkey Bizz-Ness B-17-F 8 AF AFM

My Baby B-17 42-107033 91 BG 8 AF After six months of service, failed to return from a mission to Thionville. *AFM*

Memphis Belle B-17 41-24485 8AF First B-17 to complete 25 missions. The plane and crew returned to take part in war bond drives. Shot up on numerous occasions, and bears the scars of combat. During its 25 missions, it accounted for eight enemy fighters shot down, five probables, and damage to twelve others. *NASM*

Memphis Belle The aircraft is currently being restored in Memphis, TN. *NASM*

The crew of the **Memphis Belle** during the retirement ceremony prior to returning to the states. *NASM*

Nora 2nd B-17 42-29529 96 BG 384BG 305BG 8 AF AFM

Nemesis of Aeroembolism B-17 Used in high-altitude crew testing. Aeroembolism is formation of nitrogen bubbles in the blood due to rapid altitude decompression, like the bends. *AFM*

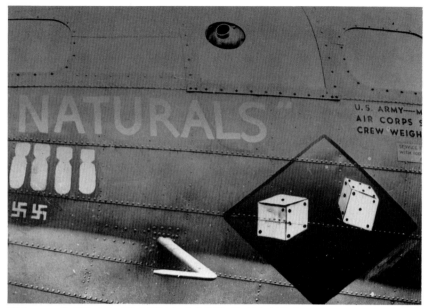

"Naturals" B-17 42-29711 94 BG 8 AF AFM

Old Glory B-17 42-31432 303 BG 8 AF Began service January 18, 1944; lost June 22, 1944. AFM

Our Bridget B-17-G 44-6975 91 BG 8 AF AFM

Out House Mouse B-17 42-31636 Joined the 91st BG, 8th AF, March 12, 1944; returned May 25, 1945. On August 16, 1944, a German 163 B rocket fighter flew alongside for 30 seconds without attacking . . . probably checking out the nose art! AFM

The Peacemaker B-17 43-37552 91 BG 8AF Began service June 2, 1944; salvaged April 13, 1945. AFM

Perpetual Help B-17 43-38887 457 BG 8 AF First named "Perpetual Hell" November 4, 1944—Note the photo taped onto the aircraft—returned to the US during May 1945. AFM

Piccadilly Lilly II B-17 42-37800 100 BG 8 AF Named for the Piccadilly Circus in London. Beyond repair June 28, 1944. *AFM*

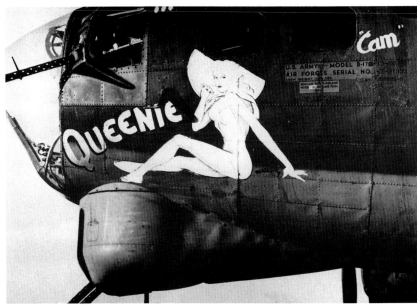

Queenie B-17 42-31353 91 BG 8 AF Began service December 20, 1943; lost over Berlin April 29, 1944. *AFM*

Raging Red B-17 42-31353 91 BG 8 AF Joined the 91st June 21, 1943; lost to Schweinfurt August 17, 1943. *AFM*

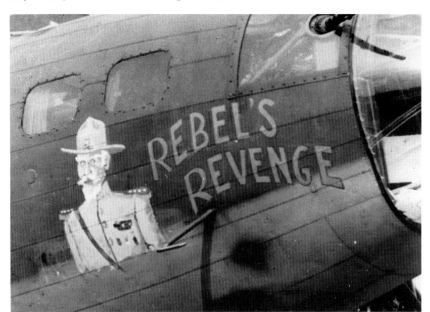

Rebel's Revenge B-17 42-29750 Joined the 91st BG, 8 AF, August 24, 1943; lost over Emden September 27, 1943. *AFM*

Rebel's Revenge In flight. *NASM*

The Red Gremlin B-17 *AFM*

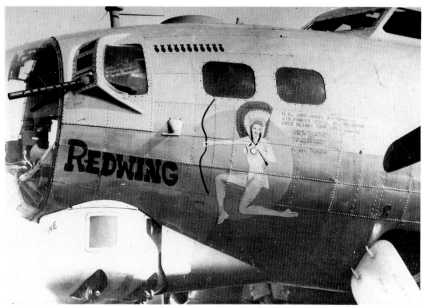

Redwing B-17 43-38088 91 BG 8 AF *AFM*

Ruby's Raiders B-17 44-6483 385 BG 9 AF This aircraft was named for Cpl. Ruby Newell of Longbeach, CA. Voted the most beautiful WAC in England. *AFM*

Royal Flush! B-17 42-6087 100 BG 8 AF Note the face of the joker and the sixteen kills for twenty bombing missions. *AFM*

Scheherazade B-17 42-29886 379 BG 8 AF Failed to return from Frankfurt January 29, 1944. *AFM*

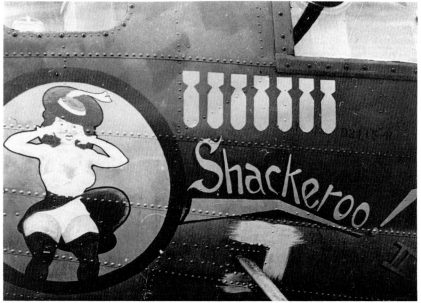

Shackeroo! II B-17 42-29708 94 BG 8 AF First assigned to the 95th BG, it was named after joining the 94th in May 1943. *AFM*

68

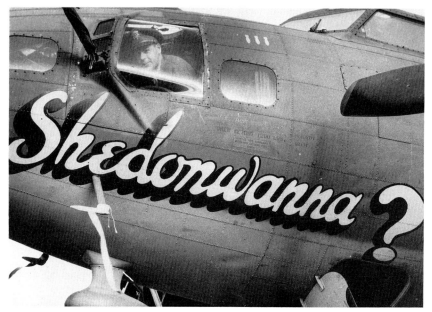

Shedonwanna? B-17 42-30201 388 BG 8 AF Lt. Baum looks out of the left front side gunners port sometime in 1943. Lost September 6, 1943, on a mission to Stuttgart. *NASM*

Snap! Crackle! Pop! B-17 41-24620 303 BG 8 AF Lost over St. Nazaire January 3, 1943. AFM

Snoozin' Suzan B-17 AFM

Stage Door Canteen B-17 42-31990 381 BG 535 BS 8 AF Christened by Mary Churchill April 23, 1944, along with George Parks, Vivien Leigh and Laurence Olivier. Flew over 100 missions before returning to the US in June 1945. AFM

Sit n Git B-26 AFM

Spirit of '44 B-17 42-37940 91BG 8AF Began service December 13, 1943; salvaged January 16, 1944. AFM

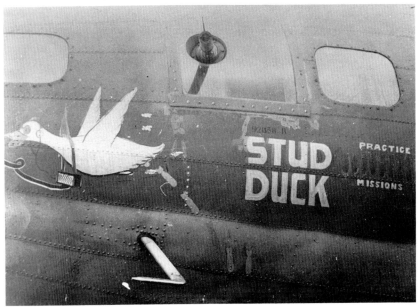

Stud Duck B-17 100 BG & 94 BG 8 AF AFM

Superman B-17 The oldest ship in the oldest group in North Africa, has had over seventeen engines, 300 flak holes and six purple hearts with no fatalities. *AFM*

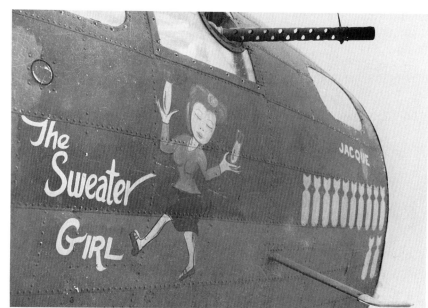

The Sweater Girl B-17 379 BG 8 AF *AFM*

Tondelayo B-17 42-29896 379 BG 8 AF Failed to return from Stuttgart September 6, 1943. *AFM*

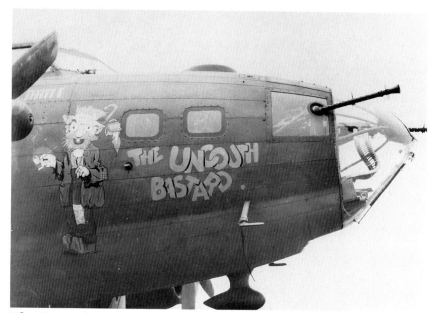

The Uncouth Bastard B-17 305 BG 8 AF *AFM*

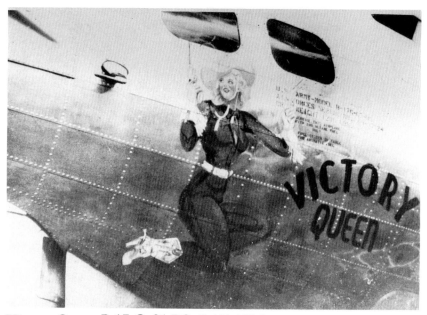

Victory Queen B-17-G 91 BG 8 AF *AFM*

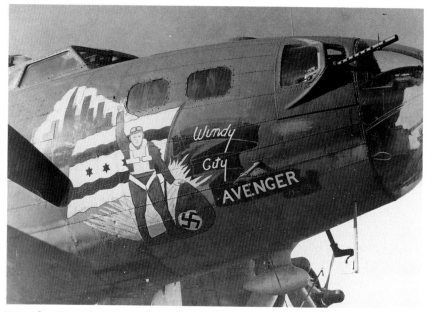

Windy City Avenger B-17 42-3037 384 BG & 305 BG 8 AF Arrived at the 384 BG September 20, 1943; declared beyond repair October 12, 1943. *AFM*

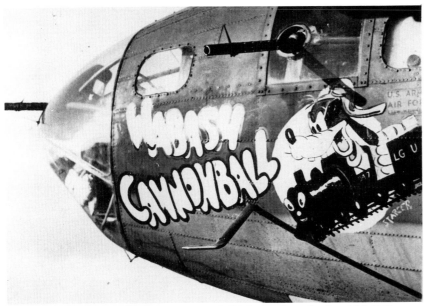

Wabash Cannonball B-17 42-29947 Served with the 100 BG, 300 BG, 91 BG, 388 BG and survived the war. AFM

Wahoo B-17-F 41-24468 369 BS 306 BG 8 AF 1st Lt. Robert P. Riordan of El Paso, TX, gives the war cry after landing with flak damage after a raid on Lillie, France. November 12, 1942. Later destroyed on landing, June 26, 1943. AFM

Mickey Mouse B-17 AFM

B-17 AFM

The Joker's Wild B-17 41-24521 AFM

General "Ike" B-17 42-97061 91BG 8 AF Note prop damage. AFM

Scarlett O'Hara B-17 379BG 8AF AFM

Bonnie-B B-17 42-31483 303BG 8AF Began service January 1, 1944; salvaged September 9, 1944. *AFM*

Dragon Lady B-17 42-30836 385 BG 8AF Lost over Pas de Calais February 13, 1944. *NASM*

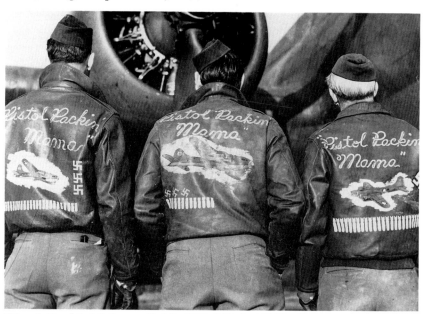

Pistol Packin' Mama B-17 390 BG 8 AF Hoffman, May and Morris display their jackets. *AFM*

100 missions, 13 ships, 5 aircraft *NASM*

Grin 'n Bare It B-17 8 AF NASM

Achin' Back NASM

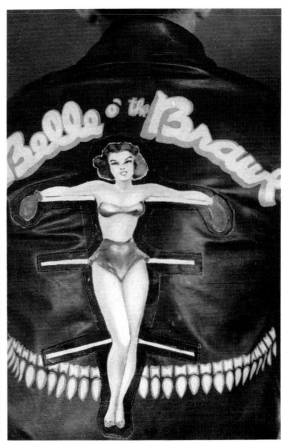

Belle O' The Brawl B-17 401 BG 8 AF NASM

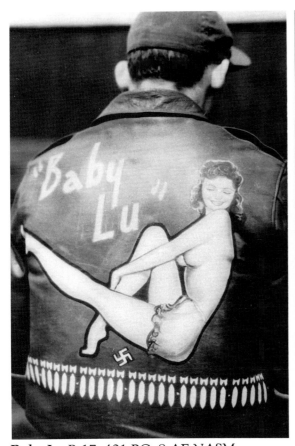

Baby Lu B-17 401 BG 8 AF NASM

Fancy Nancy B-17 401 BG 8 AF NASM

Gaposis B-17 401 BG 8 AF NASM

Grin'n Bare It B-17 8 AF NASM

Grin'n Bare It B-17 8 AF NASM

Fancy Nancy IV B-17 401 BG 8 AF NASM

Der Grossarschvogel B-17 8 AF NASM

Heavy Date B17 612 BS 401 BG 8 AF NASM

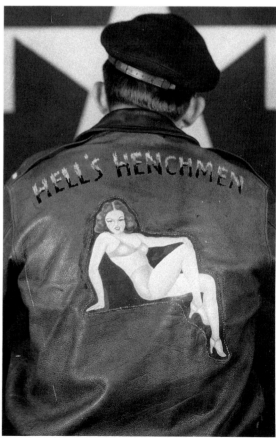

Hell's Henchmen B-17 401 BG 8 AF NASM

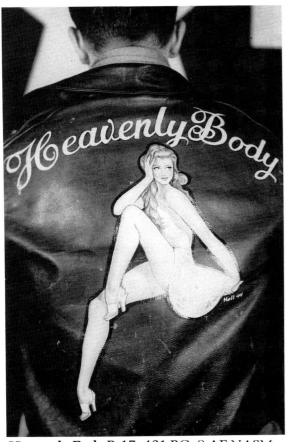

Heavenly Body B-17 401 BG 8 AF NASM

Home James B-17 457 BS 401 BG 8 AF NASM

Hi Ho Silver B-17 322BS 91 BG 8 AF NASM

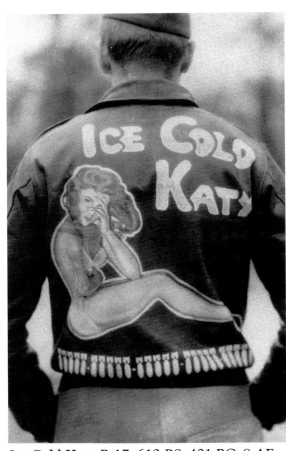

Ice Cold Katy B-17 612 BS 401 BG 8 AF NASM

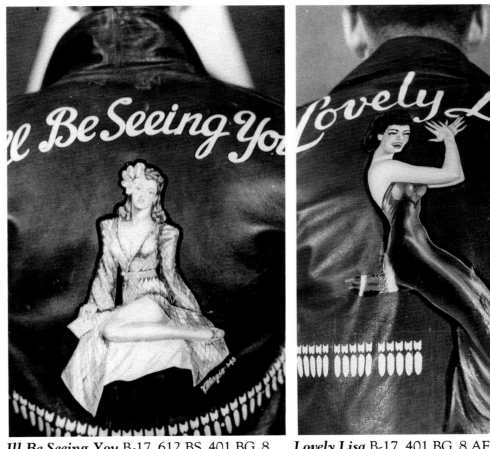

Ill Be Seeing You B-17 612 BS 401 BG 8 AF NASM

Lovely Lisa B-17 401 BG 8 AF NASM

Miss Wing Ding B-17 401 BG 8 AF NASM

Mary Alice Gnatzi-Knight B-17 401 BG 8 AF NASM

Off We Go NASM

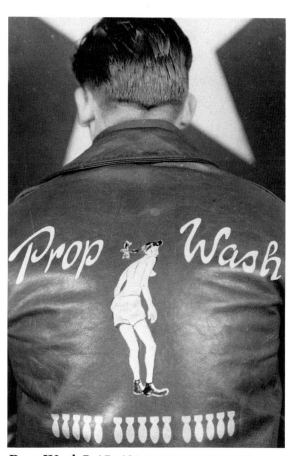

Prop Wash B-17 401 BNG 8 AF NASM

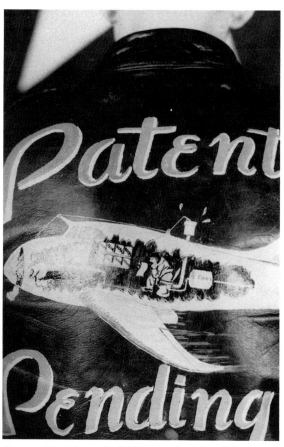

Patent Pending B-17 401 BG 8 AF NASM

Queen Sally B-17 401 BG 8 AF NASM

BTO of ETO (Big Time Operator of the European Theater of Operations) B-17 401 BG 8 AF *NASM*

Rosie's Sweat Box B-17 401 BG 8 AF *NASM*

Sweet Dreams B-17 401 BG 8 AF *NASM*

Swingin' on a Star B-17 401 BG 8 AF *NASM*

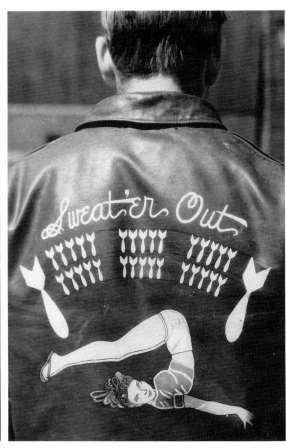

Sweat'er Out B-17 401 BG 8 AF *NASM*

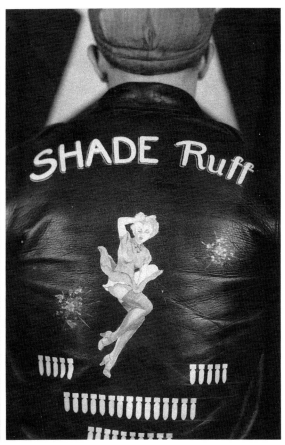

Shade Ruff B-17 401 BG 8 AF *NASM*

Snicklefritz NASM

Screamin' Demon B-17 401 BG 8A F
NASM

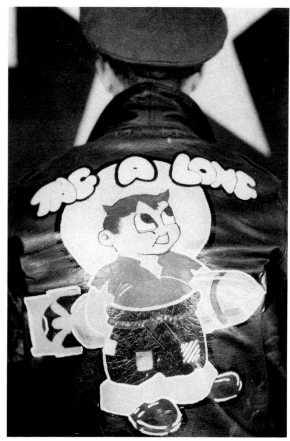

Tag A Long B-17 8 AF NASM

Twannggg B-17 NASM

Time'll Tell! NASM

Twang-g-g B-17 NASM

The Careful Virgin NASM

Visibility Perfect B-17 401 BG 8 AF NASM

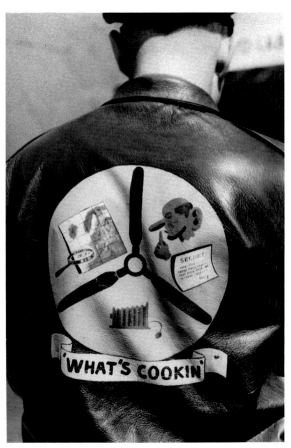

What's Cookin B-17 401 BG 8 AF NASM

Yankee Eagle NASM

Madame Queen B-17 401 BG 8 AF AFM

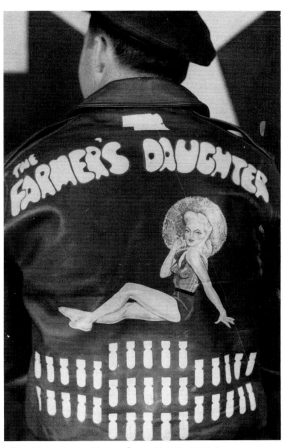

The Farmer's Daughter B-17 AFM

Hell's Angel Out of Chute 13 B-17 401
BG 8AF NASM

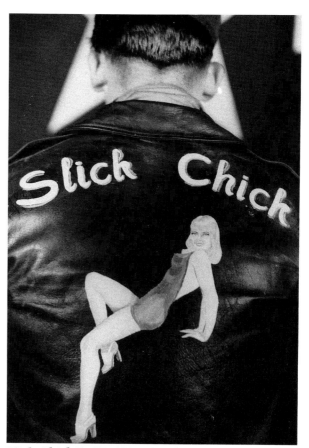

Slick Chick B-17 401 BG 8AF AFM

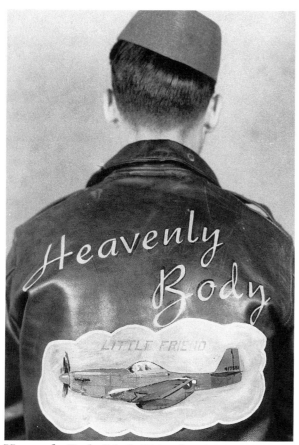

Heavenly Body-Little Friend P-51 AFM

Fitch's Bandwagon B-17 401 BG 8 AF
AFM

Just Once More B-17-G 44-8854 94 BG 333 BS 8 AF CAF/G. *Valant*

Major Byron Trent in front of *Just Once More* at Rougham, England, 1945. *B. Trent*

CAF collection

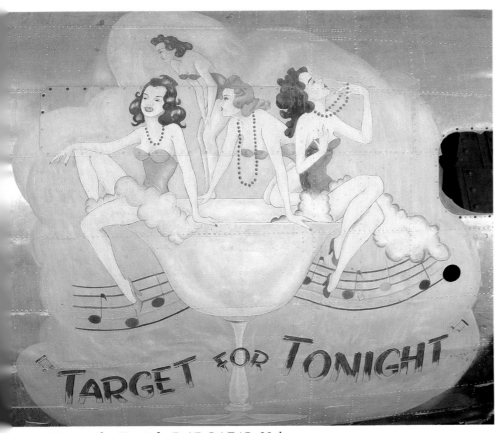

Target for Tonight B-17 CAF/G. *Valant*

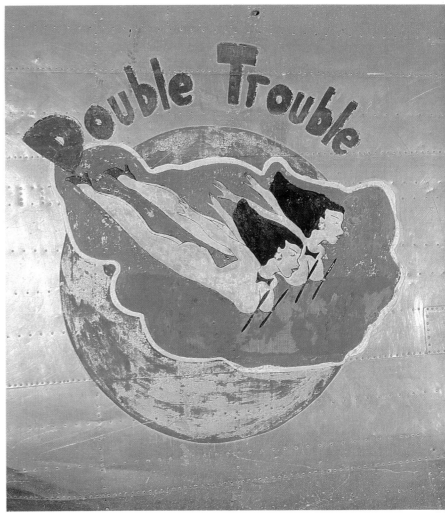

Double Trouble B-24 44-42460 436 BS 7 BG 10 AF The crew formed in March 1944 at Hammer Field, Fresno, CA, and took B-24 training at Muros AFB. They were assigned to the CBI theater in India. This is the plane that bombed the bridge over the River Kwai. CAF/G. *Valant*

Sloppy But Safe B-24 44-41008 727 BS 451 BG 15 AF CAF/G. Valant

Hump Time B-24-M-15-CO 44-42117 CAF/G. Valant

Easy Maid PB4Y privateer 42-38873 CAF/G. Valant

Flamin Mamie B-24 CAF/G. Valant

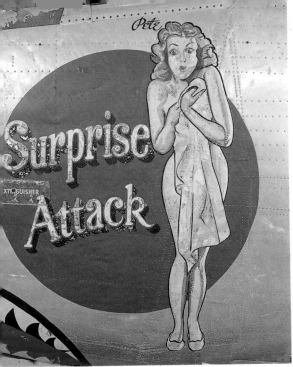

Surprise Attack B-24-M 44-50956 374 BS 308 BG 14 AF CAF/G. Valant

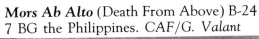

Mors Ab Alto (Death From Above) B-24 7 BG the Philippines. CAF/G. Valant

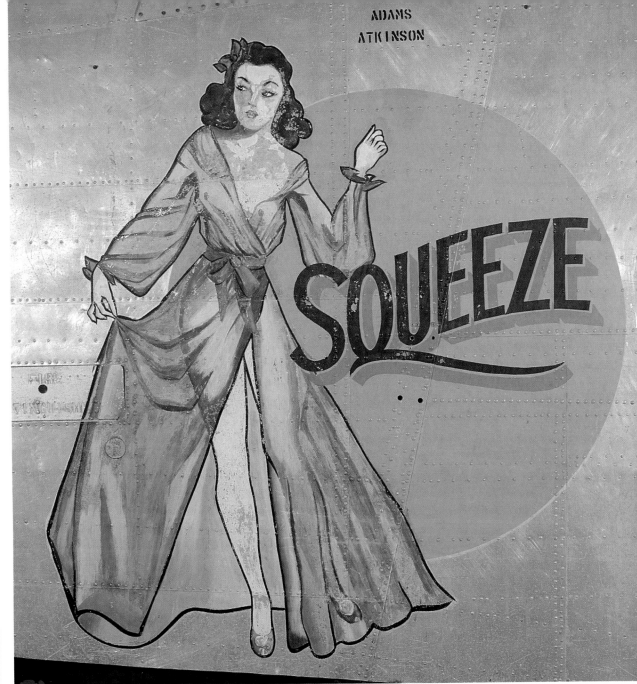

Squeeze B-24-M 44-420200 374 BS 308 BG 14 AF CAF/G. Valant

Mama Foo Foo B-24-M 44-42094 374 BS 308 BG 14 AF CAF/G. Valant

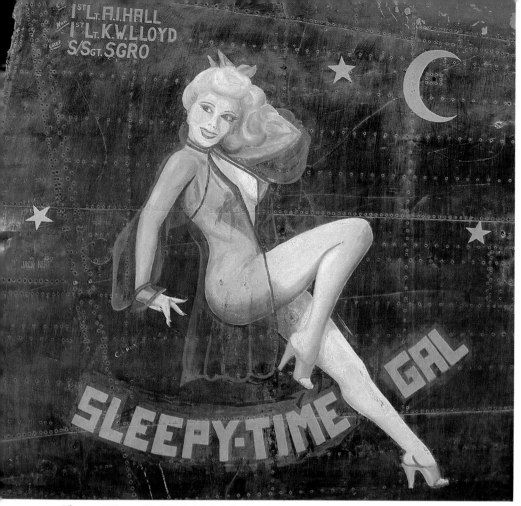

Sleepy Time Gal B-24-M-15 44-51030 CAF/G. Valant

Home Stretch B-24 7 BG 10 AF CAF/G. Valant

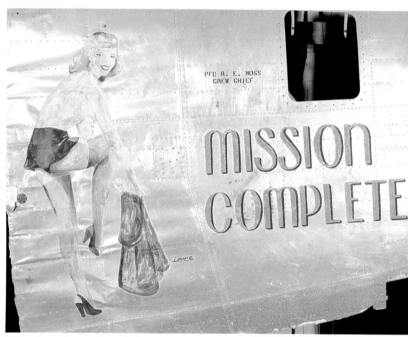

Mission Completed B-17 CAF/G. Valant

Yellow Fever B-24-M 44-50803 374 BS 308 BG 14 AF
CAF/G. Valant

Forever Amber B-24-J 42-73188 374 BS 308 BG 14 AF CAF/G.
Valant

You Speak B-24 454 BG 737 BS 15 AF
Italy. CAF/G. Valant

Lassie I'm Home B-17 7 BG 436 BS 10 AF CAF/G. Valant

Miss Yourlovin B-24 CAF/G. Valant

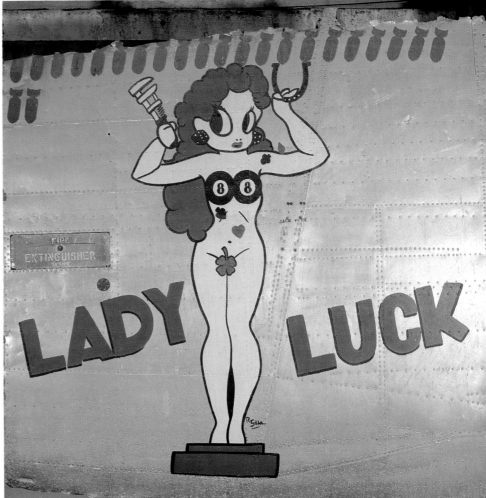

Lady Luck B-24 CAF/G. Valant

85

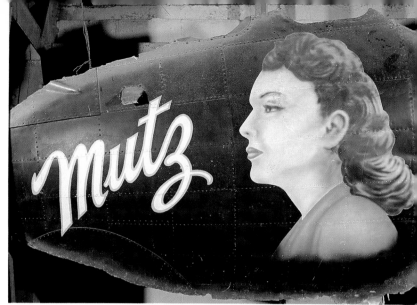

Mutz CAF/G. Valant

Nobby's Harriet J B-17 CAF/G. Valant

B-17 CAF/G. Valant

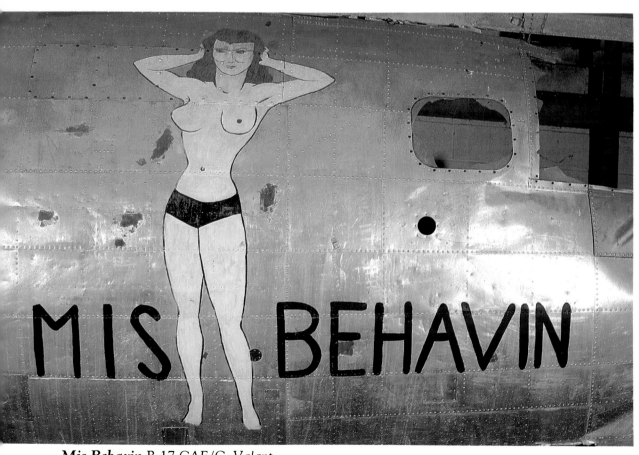

Mis Behavin B-17 CAF/G. Valant

CAF/G. Valant

Yankee Girl B-16 42-7522 506 BS 44 BG CAF/G. Valant

B-17-G 44-6779 CAF/G. Valant

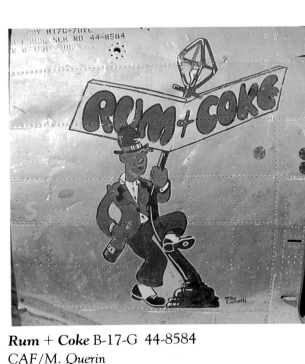

Rum + Coke B-17-G 44-8584
CAF/M. Querin

Southern Comfort CAF/G. Valant

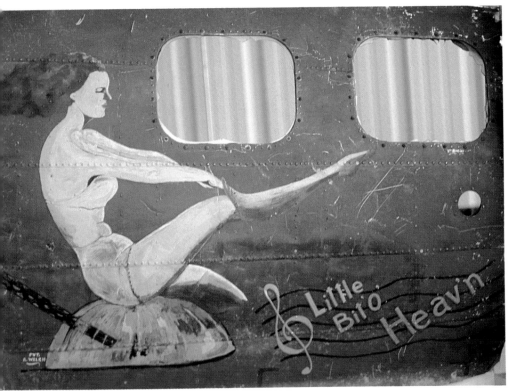

Little Bit'O' Heav'n B-17 CAF/M. Querin

Brinkman working on **Aries** B-24 42-52693 486 BG 834 BS 8 AF C. Simonsen/M. Brown

Clarence Simonsen's color painting of Brinkman's **Taurus.** C. Simonsen/G. Valant

Brinkman nose art

Gemini B-24 41-29490 486 BG 834 BS 8 AF Brinkman artwork. C. Simonsen/M. Brown

Virgo B-24 42-52532 486 BG 834 BS 8 AF Brinkman artwork. C. Simonsen/M. Brown

Leo B-24 486 BG 834 BS 8 AF Brinkman artwork. C.S./M artwork. *C. Simonsen/M. Brown*

Libra B-24 42-52508 486 BG 834 BS 8 AF Brinkman nose art. *C. Simonsen/M. Brown*

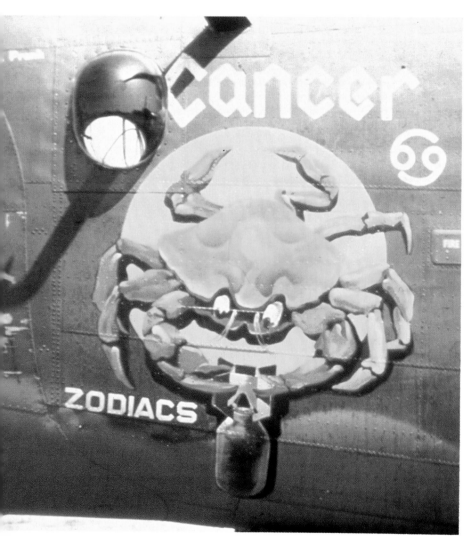

Cancer B-24 42-52665 486 BG 834 BS 8 AF Brinkman artwork. *C. Simonsen/M. Brown*

Varga Girls

Night Mission B-24-D 42-40891 Was assigned to the 397 bombardment squadron and patrolled from Managua to Salinas, Ecuador, and all over the Caribbean. *Esquire.* CAF/G. Valant

"O-O-Nothing!" B-24 *Esquire.* CAF/M. Querin

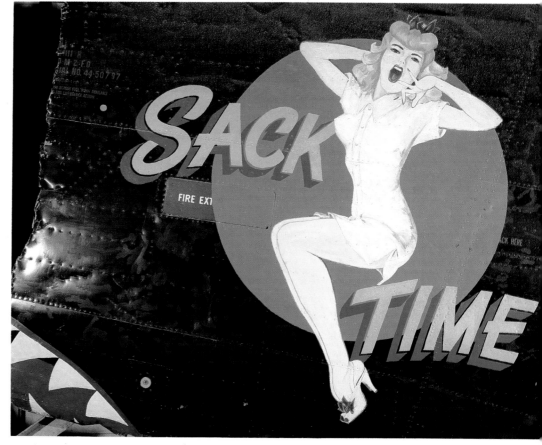

Sack Time B-24-M 44-50797 308 BG *Esquire.* CAF/G. Valant

Ole Baldy B-24 8 AS *C. Simonsen*

Bobby Sox B-17-G 44-8158 94 BG 332 BS 8 AF *C. Simonsen*

Miss Manchester B-26-C 320 BG 441 BS The crest was "unofficial" and used in World War II only. *C. Simonsen*

Belle Ringer B-26-C 320 BG 441 BS C. *Simonsen*

Tondelayo B-24 487 BG 8 AF Artist: Sgt. Daune Bryers C. *Simonsen*

Old Rusty P-38 1st FTR GP Pilot W. G. Campbell. C. *Simonsen*

Bonnie P-47 56 FTR GP 61 FTR SQN 8 AF C. *Simonsen*

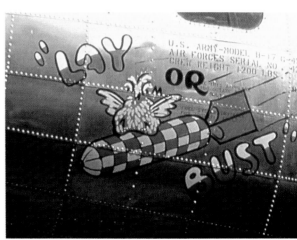

Lay or Bust B-17-G 42-97230 100 BG
C. Simonsen

Miss Barbara B-17-F 41-24519 AFM

Our Gal Sal B-17-G 42-31767 100 BG Scrapped at Kingman,
AZ, 1947. C. Simonsen

P-47 318 FTR GP 333 FTR SQN C. Simonsen

Shady Lady B-24 44-40439 8 AF
C. Simonsen

Peace Maker B-29 19 BG C. Simonsen

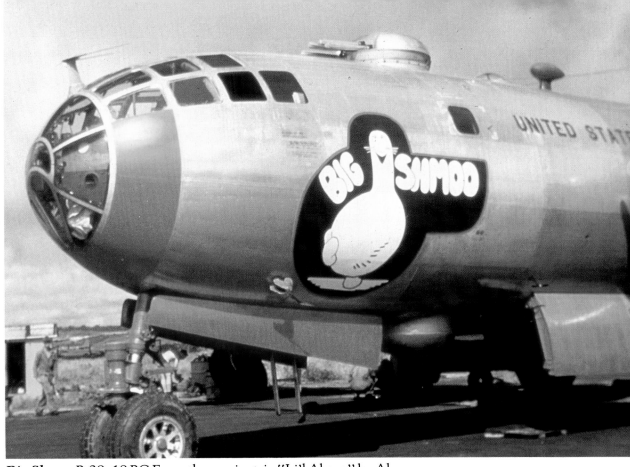

Big Shmoo B-29 19 BG From the comic strip "Li'l Abner" by Al Capp. C. Simonsen

Southern Comfort B-29 19 BG C. Simonsen

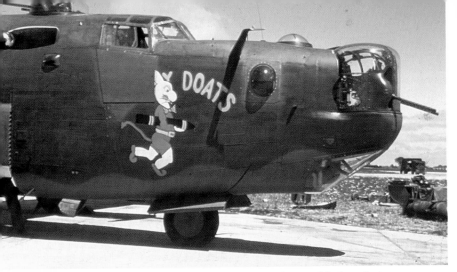

Mairzy Doates B-24 8 AF Armour plate added to help protect the pilot covers a portion of the original artwork. *C. Simonsen*

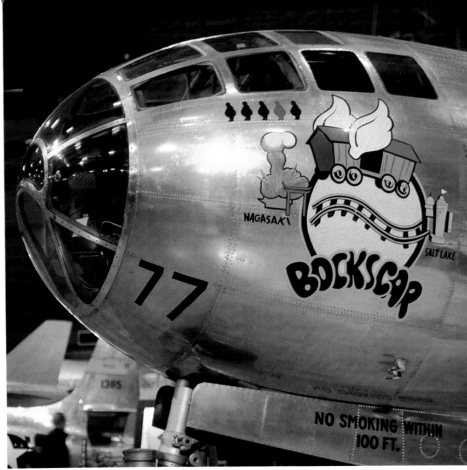

Bockscar B-29 Second plane to drop an atomic bomb on Japan, it is in the Air Force Museum, Dayton, Ohio. *AFM/G. Valant*

Senta A Pua *NASM*

Finito Benito Next Hirohito B-25 Photo taken over Italy. *NASM*

The "Goon" B-24 NASM

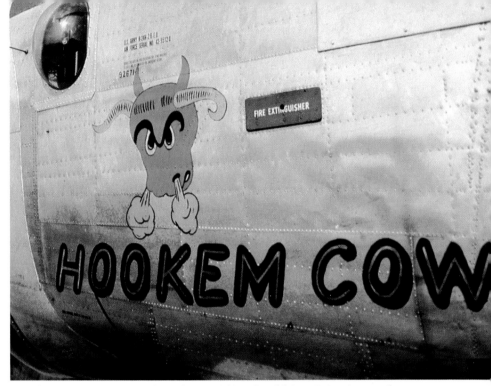

Hookem Cow B-24-H 42-95128 458 BG 755 BS 8 AF Artwork by Harold Johnston. Crashed April 14, 1945. NASM

NASM

This restored P-40 hangs in the National Air and Space Museum, Washington, D.C. NASM/G. Valant

Wash's Tub B-24 NASM

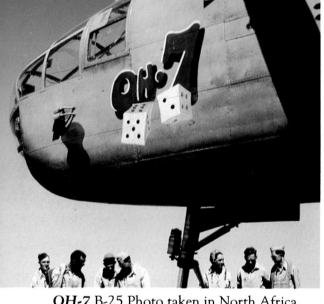

OH-7 B-25 Photo taken in North Africa. NASM

Idiots' Delight B-17 42-30301 94 BG 8 AF NASM

Alabama Express B-26 NASM

Willit Run? Restored P-51 at the National Air and Space Museum. NASM/G. *Valant*

Lonesome Polecat Jr B-24 China. NASM

Little Miss Mischief B-17 42-97880 91 BG 8 AF Nose art painted by Tony Starcer, who did over 130 aircraft. Crash landing April 1945, Bassingbourn, England. NASM

5 Grand B-17 43-37716 96 BG 8AF. The 5,000th B-17 produced by Boeing after Pearl Harbor. It was signed by the factory workers and flew in combat as shown. It survived the war, but not the smelters; it was scrapped at Kingman, AZ, in 1947. The plane had "5 Grand" painted on both sides of the nose, but the crew called her "Easter Egg." *NASM*

Pappy Recon plane with Li'l Abner's Pappy sitting under a B-17 in England. *NASM*

Schnozzle B-17-G-1Q-VE 42-45611 381 BG 8 AF Began with 381st January 22, 1944; salvaged November 27, 1944. *NASM*

Ferocious Frankie P-51 Lt. Col. Wallace Hopkins flies over
England. *NASM*

Tom Paine B-17-F 42-30790 388 BG 8
AF *NASM*

Lou IV and other P-51s fly deep escort for B-17s over Germany.
Note the extra fuel tanks under the wings. These could be released
for air combat. *NASM*

Fifinella B-17 8 AF The name Fifinella means female gremlin.
The first Fifinella was reported at Kelly Field, TX, around 1923.
The RAF saw the first one in England in 1928, and since then every
Air Force in the world has had them. Flyers claim that gremlins live
near airports and like to collect nuts and bolts from aircraft. There
are a few good gremlins, but we fear that most are bad, as they tend
to steal important nuts and bolts. The Fifinella are exceptionally
beautiful and live off the pimento stuffing found in martini olives,
which give them the delicate complexions. *NASM*

B-24s form up on a lead ship. Note the colorful markings on the
lead ship. After the formation was set, the lead ship (usually a tired
veteran) would return to base. *NASM*

B-17s with fighter escort somewhere over Europe. *NASM*

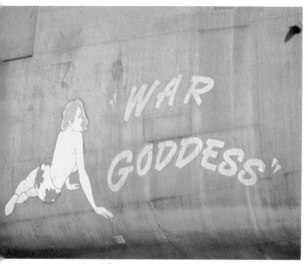

War Goddess B-24 93BG 8AF AFM

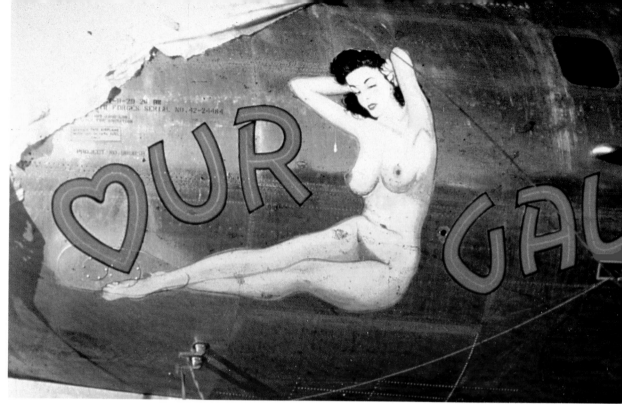

Our Gal B-29 42-24484 AFM

B-17 over England NASM

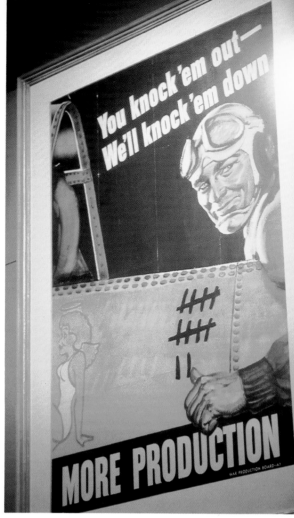

Dream Girl Restored A-26 "Invader" at the Air Force Museum. AFM/*G. Valant*

World War II production poster as it hangs in the Air Force Museum at Dayton, Ohio. Note the nose art. AFM/*G. Valant*

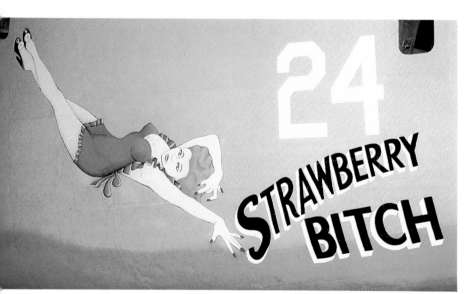

Strawberry Bitch B-24 Painted in US prior to going to North Africa. Now in the Air Force Museum. AFM/*H. V. Morgan*

Boulder Buff B-24 AFM

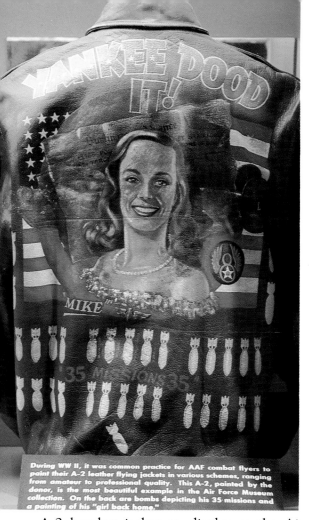

During WW II, it was common practice for AAF combat flyers to paint their A-2 leather flying jackets in various schemes, ranging from amateur to professional quality. This A-2, painted by the donor, is the most beautiful example in the Air Force Museum collection. On the back are bombs depicting his 35 missions and a painting of his "girl back home."

A-2 bomber jacket on display at the Air Force Museum. *AFM*

This artwork was done in Oklahoma City prior to departure for the South Pacific. *AFM*

Beat Up Bastard (Bub for short) B-29 19 BG R. Mann

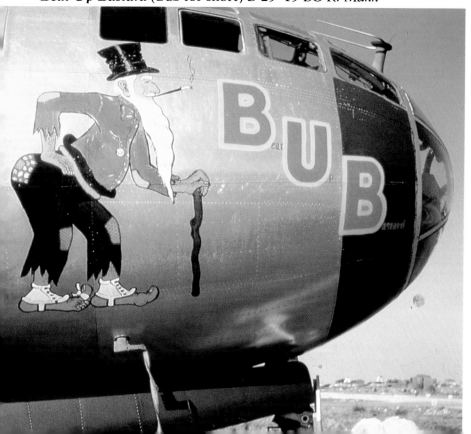

Never Hoppen B-29 19 BG R. Mann

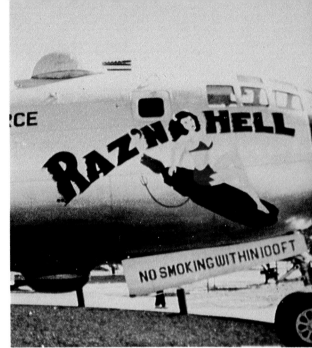

Raz'n Hell B-29 *R. Mann*

South Sea Sinner B-29 19 BG *R. Mann*

No Sweat B-29 19 BG Aircraft lost, date unknown. *R. Mann*

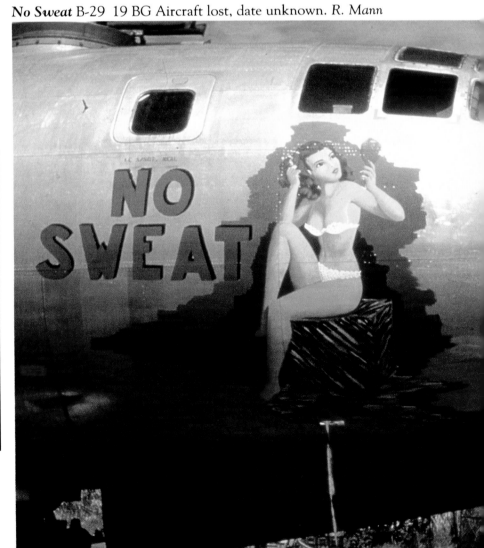

Miss N.C. B-29 19 BG *R. Mann*

This is real nose art. CAF/G. Valant

Bugs (Ball) Buster B-29 19 BG R. Mann

Censored Cream of the Crop B-29 19 BG R. Mann

Restored P-40 of the Confederate Air Force—Harlingen, Texas.
CAF/G. Valant

Queen of Hearts B-24 *Tim Bivens*

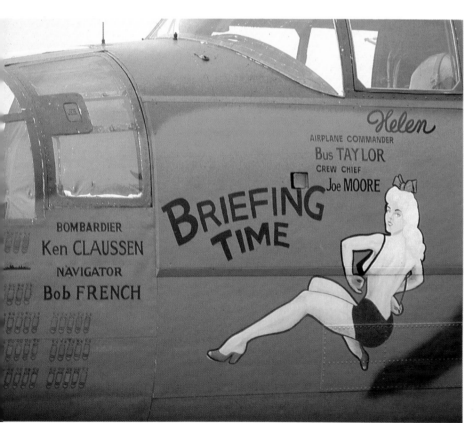

Briefing Time B-25 43-27638 57 BW 340 BG 489 BS This
restored B-25 flew in North Africa and Italy. It is presently owned
by the Mid Atlantic Air Museum, which did the restoration.
MAAM/G. Valant

Draggin' Lady This C-47 flies with CAF. Note one downed
aircraft credit. CAF/G. Valant

Special Delivery This B-25 flies out of Houston, TX, and is owned by R. L. Waltrip. *G. Valant*

Yellow Rose Contemporary nose art on a B-25. *CAF/G. Valant*

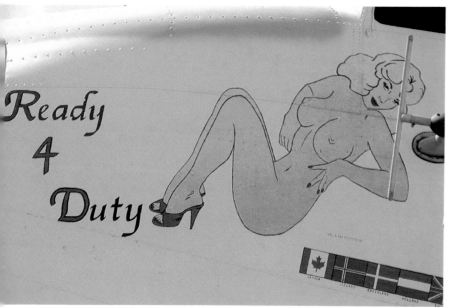

Ready 4 Duty C-47 *CAF/G. Valant*

Texas Raiders Contemporary nose art on this CAF B-17. *CAF/G. Valant*

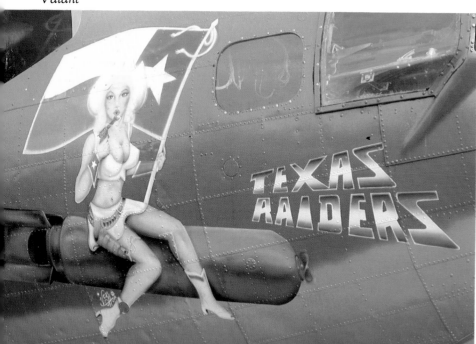

Diamond Lil Started life as a B-24, but was damaged on its way to England. Converted to a C-87 cargo plane, it flew all over the US during the war. Obtained by the CAF. It has been partially converted back to a B-24. *CAF/G. Valant*

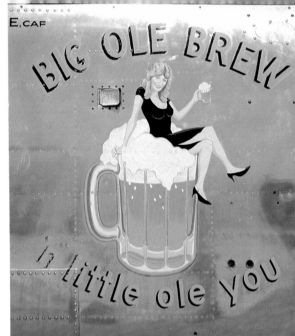

Big Ole Brew N Little Ole You B-25
CAF/G. Valant

Sentimental Journey B-17 CAF/G. Valant

Daisy Mae Contemporary nose art on a B-25. CAF/G. Valant

The Black Sparrow A CAF C-47 CAF/G. Valant

Undecided F-111 Nose art is on the way back. USAF/G. Valant

Lucky Strike F-111 This artwork also flew on a B-24 in the Philippines in 1944. USAF/G. Valant

Dragon Lady B-24 C. Simonsen

Cocktail Hour B-24-J-161-CO 44-40428 43BG 403 BS C. Simonsen

The Shack B-24-J-CO-156 44-40398 753 BS 487 BG Painted by Burne Bryers. *C. Simonsen*

A Bit o' Lace B-17-G-40-VE 42-97976 709 BS 447 BG Painted by Nicholas Fingelly from a sketch by Milton Caniff. Miss Lace was a character in Caniff's "Male Call," which ran in the army camp newspapers. Miss Lace became a favorite character with the GIs because she preferred enlisted men to officers, but called them "General" or "Admiral." Another Caniff character that was widely copied was "the Dragon Lady." *C. Simonsen*

Salem's Angel A fragment of an A-2 jacket. *M. Warro*

Little Cheezer B-17 401 BG 8 AF AFM

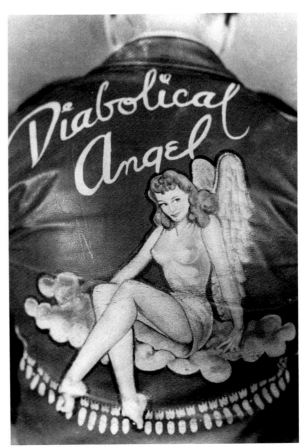

Diabolical Angel B-17 401 BG 612 BS 8 AF AFM

Veni-Vidi-Vici B-17 401 BG 8 AF AFM

Tantalizing Takeoff B-17 AFM

A-Vailable B-24 NASM

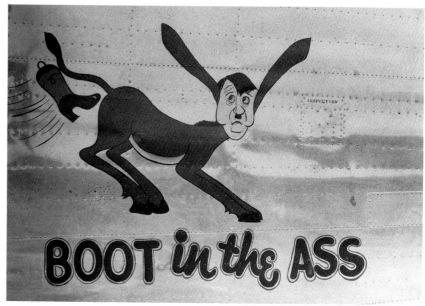

Boot in the Ass B-24 AFM

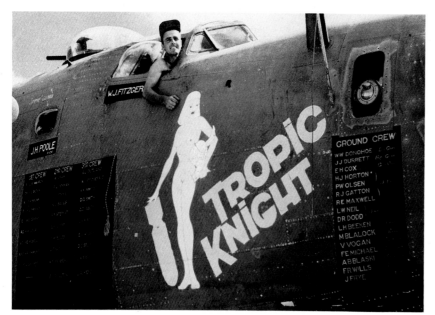

Tropic Knight B-24 Note crew lists. NASM

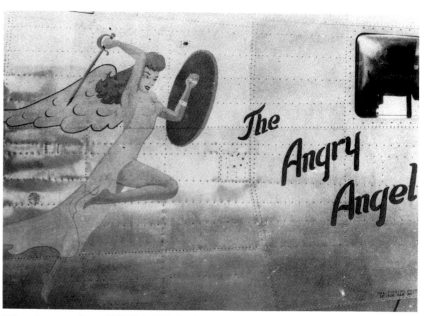

The Angry Angel B-24 7 BG 9 BS 10 AF *Leo Huken*

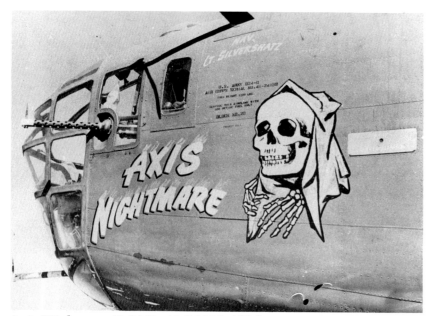

Axis Nightmare B-24-D 41-24138 AFM

Snow White and the Seven Dwarfs B-24 343 BS 98 BG 9 AF
NASM

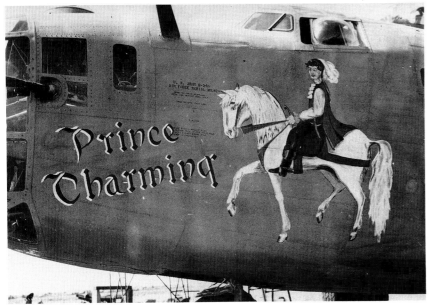

Prince Charming B-24-D 343 BS 98 BG 9 AF NASM

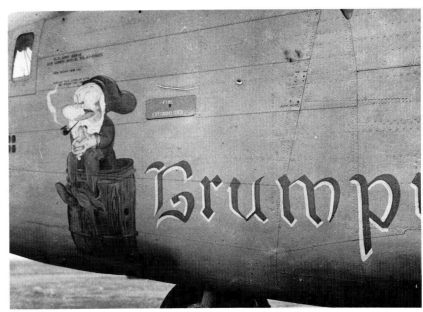

Grumpy B-24-D 42-41825 343 BS 98 BG 9AF AFM

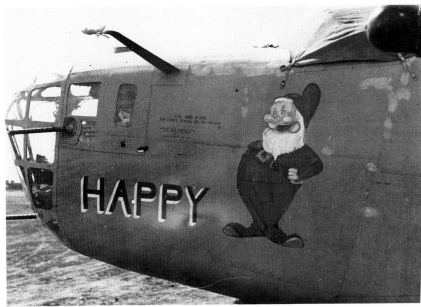

Happy B-24-D 42-40256 343 BS 98 BG 9 AF AFM

Sneezy B-24-D 41-3795 343 BS 98 BG 9 AF AFM

Sleepy B-24-D 41-11701 343 BS 98 BG 9 AF AFM

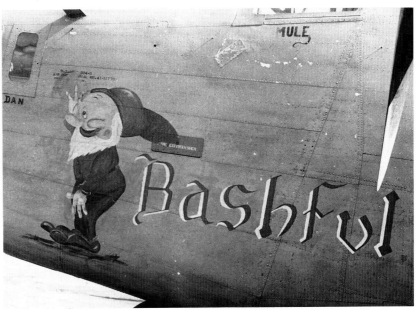

Bashful B-24-D 41 11770 343 BS 98 BG 99 AF AFM

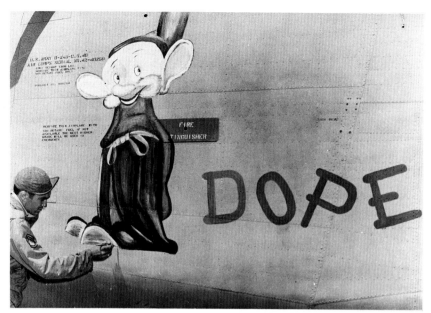

Dopey B-24-D 42-40268 343 BS 98 BG 9 AF AFM

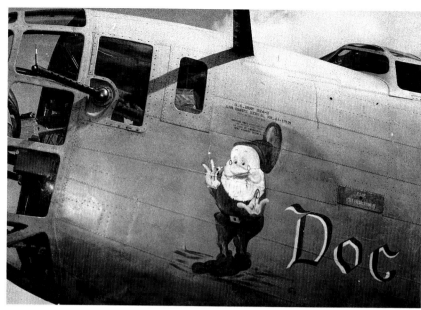

Doc B-24-D 41-11921 343 BS 98 BG 9 AF NASM

The Witch B-24-D 1-11834 343 BS 98 BG 9 AF Note mission symbols. AFM

Big Time Operator B-24-J 44-40737 AFM

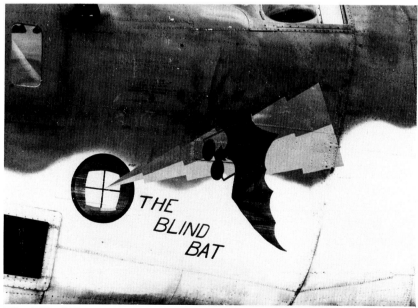

The Blind Bat B-24-D 42-11738 AFM

Bodacious Critter B-24 AFM

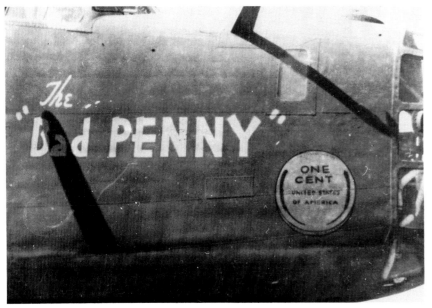

The Bad Penny B-24 AFM

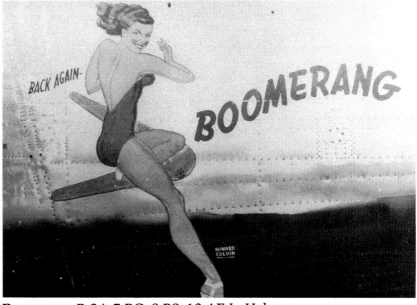

Boomerang B-24 7 BG 9 BS 10 AF *L. Huken*

Balls o' Fire B-25 AFM

Buzzzz Job B-24 AFM

Bourbon Boxcar B-24 AFM

Barbara Jean B-24 AFM

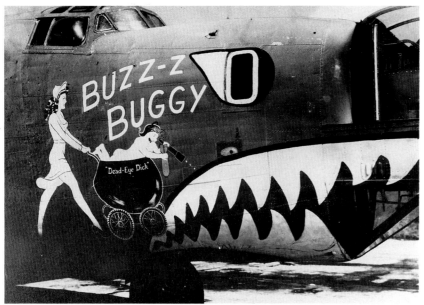

Buzz-z Buggy B-24 374 BS 308 BG Chengkung China aircraft destroyed in a taxiing accident. *AFM*

"Bottoms Up" B-24 *AFM*

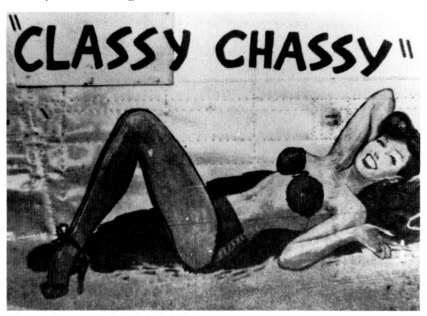

Classy Chassy B-24 8 AF *AFM*

Cherokee Strip B-24 20th combat mapping squad. *AFM*

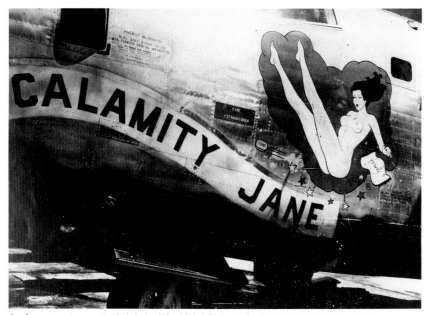

Calamity Jane B-24-M 44-42019 7 BG 9 BS 10 AF *L. Huken*

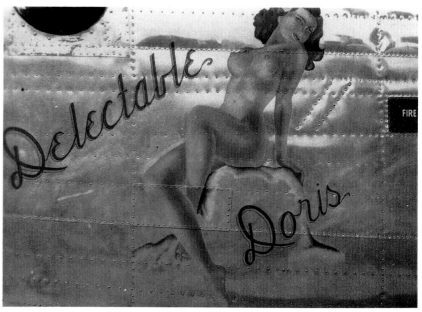

Delectable Doris B-24-J 42-50551 566 BS 389 BG 8 AF *T. Bivens*

Dragon Lady B-24 AFM

The Dragon and his Tail B-24 Note: the tail ran the entire length of the ship. AFM

Doodlebug B-24-G 41-24223 AFM

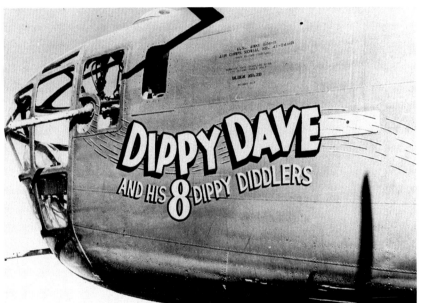

Dippy Dave and his 8 Dippy Diddlers B-24-D 41-24143 AFM

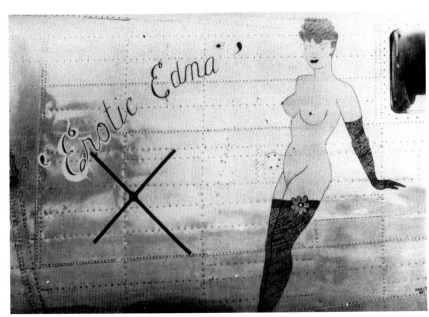

Erotic Edna B-24 7 BG 9 BS 10 AF L. Huken

Fabulous Fannie B-24 7 BG 9 BS 10 AF L. Huken

Final Objective B-24 AFM

Feathermerchant's Folly B-24 AFM

Flying Fannie B-24 AFM

Glamouras' B-24 Pronounced "Glamour Ass" AFM

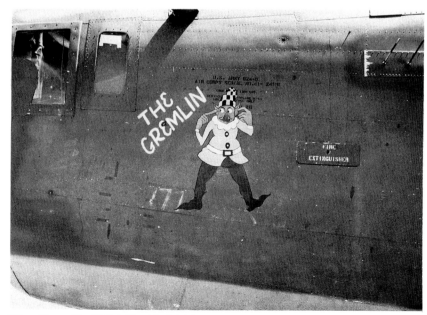

The Gremlin B-24-D 41-24111 AFM

Gang Bang B-24 C. P. Dicecco

"Hot" To Go B-24 7 BG 9 BS 10 AF L. Huken

Hilo Hattie B-24 AFM

It Aint So Funny B-24 NASM

Innocent Infant B-24-L 44-49649 308 BG AFM

Jezebelle B-24 AFM

Jungle Queen AL 640 6 BG AFM

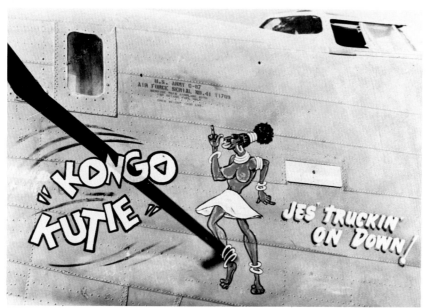

Kongo Kutie C-87 (Cargo B-24) 9th AF AFM

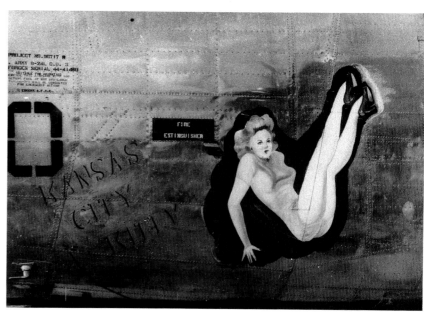

Kansas City Kitty B-24-L 44-41480

King's X B-24 AFM

"Little Flower" B-24 AFM

Lonesome Lady B-24 AFM

Luscious Lace B-24 7 BG 9 BS 10 AF *L. Huken*

Lili Marlene B-24 AFM

Munda Belle B-24 AFM

Miss Carriage B-24-D AFM

Marlene B-24 AFM

Miss Dorothy B-24 AFM

Miss Lace B-24 AFM

Miss Tennessee B-24 7 BG 9 BS 10 AF *L. Huken*

Miss Liberty B-24 *AFM*

Miss Beryl B-24 308 BG *AFM*

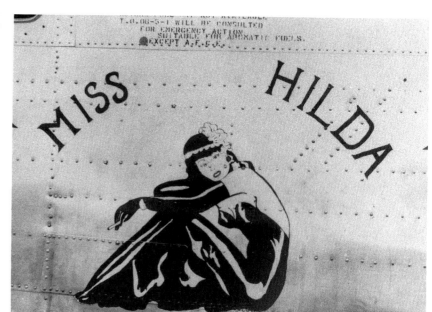

Miss Hilda B-24 7 BG 9 BS 10 AF *L. Huken*

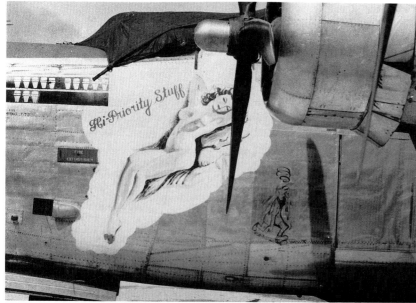

Hi Priority Stuff B-24-J 44-40967 Photo recon. Note cameras for mission markers. *AFM*

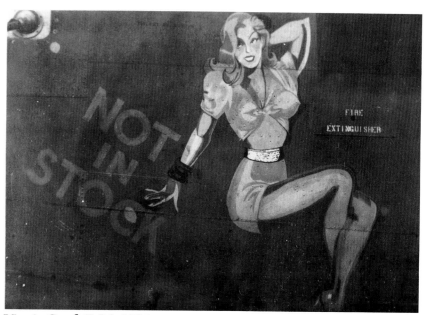

Not in Stock B-24 *AFM*

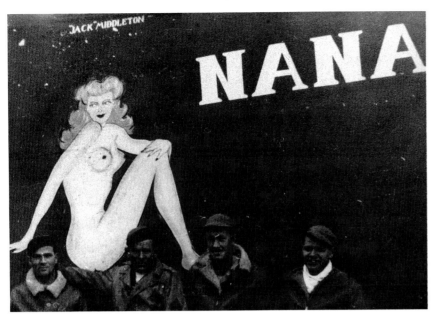

Nana B-24 566 BS 389 BG T. Bivens

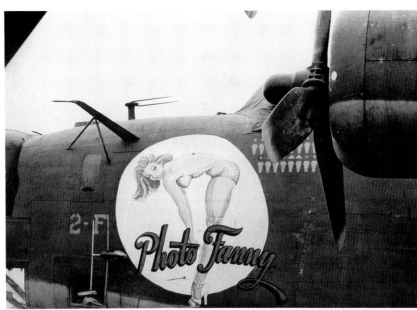

Photo Fanny B-24 Photo recon. AFM

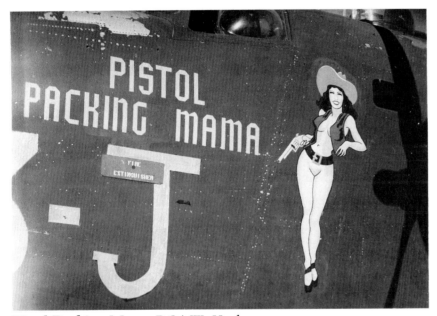

Pistol Packing Mama B-24 W. Hughs

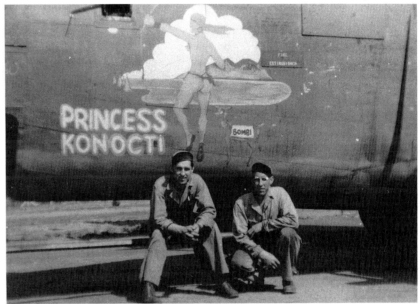

Princess Konocti B-24 566 BS 389 BG Note "Bombi" the fawn.
T. Bivens

Princess Konocti B-24 566 BS 389 BG The other side of the
plane. T. Bivens

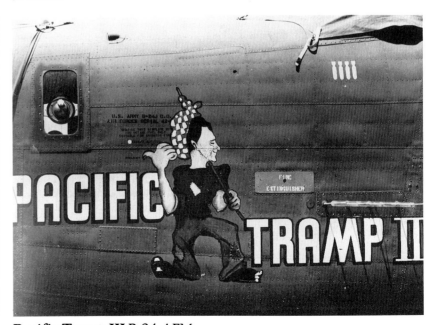

Pacific Tramp III B-24 AFM

Pappy's Passion B-24 AFM

Pacific Passion B-24 AFM

Patched Up Piece B-24 Photo recon. AFM

The Peter Heater B-24 AFM

Queen Mae B-24

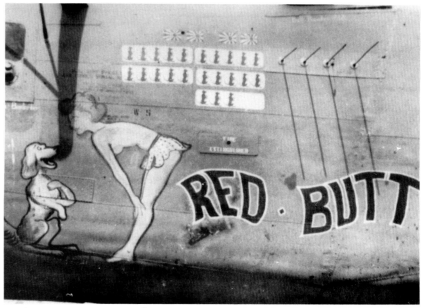

Red Butt B-24 W. Hughs

The Rip Snorter B-24 20th combat mapping squad. *AFM*

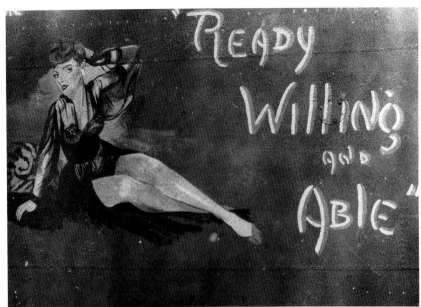

Ready Willing and Able B-24-D 41-41078 Shot down over Nadzab, crew bailed out safely. *Albert Marston*

Sweetest of Texas B-24 *AFM*

Sluggin' Sal B-24 *AFM*

Sitting Pretty B-24 *AFM*

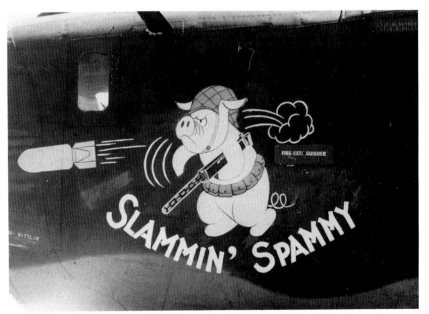

Slammin' Spammy B-24 Named in honor of the GI's favorite food—Spam. *AFM*

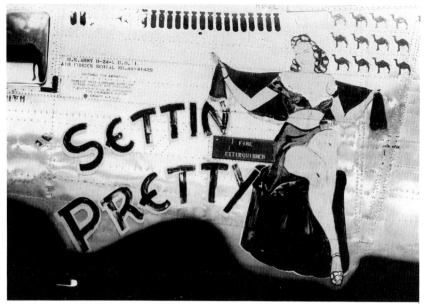

Settin Pretty B-24-L 44-41429 308 BG Note the camels that denote each trip "over the hump" (over the Himalayas). *AFM*

Satan's Baby B-24 *AFM*

Short Run! B-24 *AFM*

Tepee Time Gal B-24 *AFM*

Tennessee Belle B-24 *AFM*

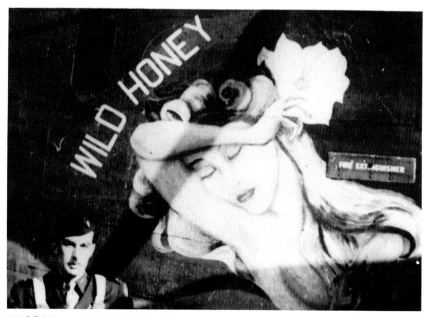

Wild Honey B-24 *W. Hughs*

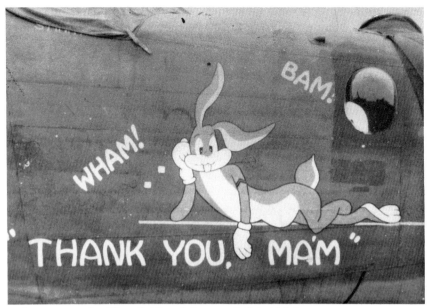

Wham! Bam! "Thank You Ma'm" B-24 AFM

Wolf Pack B-24 AFM

The Wango Wango Bird B-24 Note exhaust note. AFM

The Wolf B-24 AFM

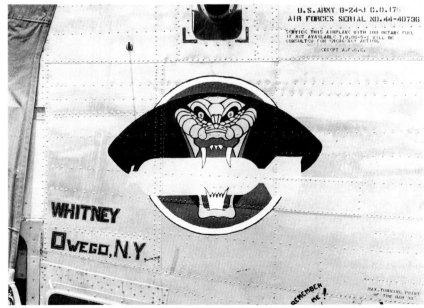

B-24-J 44-40796 This is a squadron marker. Note the instruction at the air access port "Remember Me." *AFM*

B-24 Nose art in progress. *W. Hughs*

B-24 Vargas-inspired nose art. *AFM*

B-24 **Before** *C. P. Dicecco*

B-24 **After** (other side of plane). *C. P. Dicecco*

Mission Belle B-24-D 42-40389 400 BS Nose art in progress. *AFM*

A-Tisket A-Tasket A G-I Casket B-24 Somewhere in the South Pacific; armorers prepare frag bombs for loading. *NASM*

As-cend Charlie B-24 *NASM*

Alfred II B-24 NASM

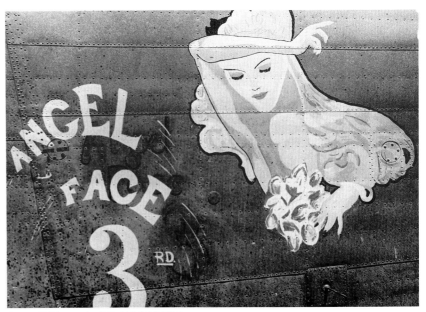

Angel Face 3rd B-24 NASM

Arkansas Traveler B-24 NASM

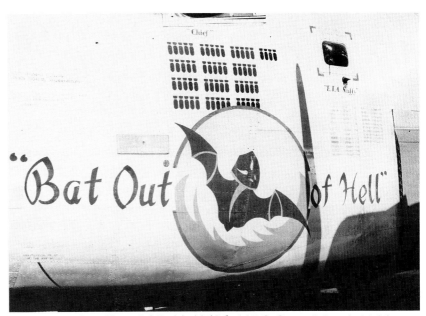

"Bat Out of Hell" B-24-J 44-40526 11BG Guam May 4, 1945. NASM

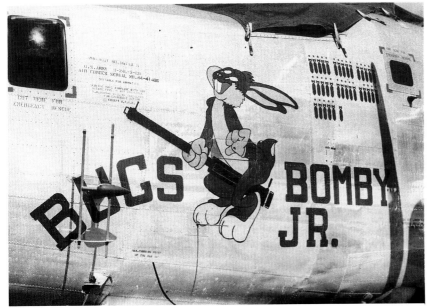

Bugs Bomby Jr. B-24-L-5-CO 44-41466 11 BG Guam. NASM

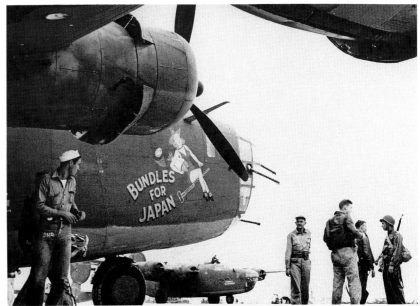

Bundles for Japan B-24 Note witch's broom is a 50-cal. machine gun. NASM

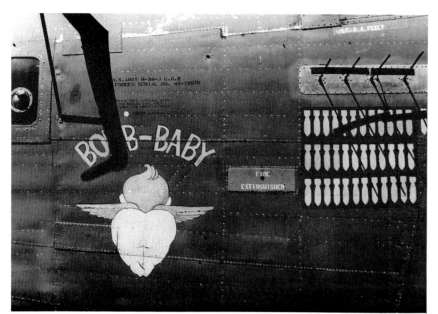

Bomb Baby B-24-J 42-72976 Photo taken on Kwajalein July 1944. *NASM*

Baby Bug B-24 490 BG 8 AF *NASM*

Barrel House Bessie B-24 July 1944. *NASM*

Battling Hornet B-24 Kwajalein July 1944. *NASM*

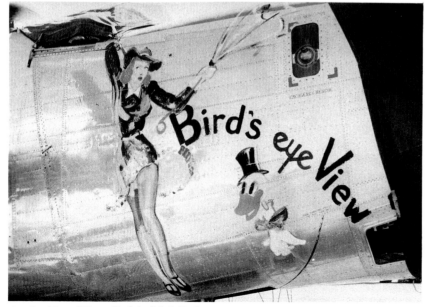

Bird's Eye View B-24 11 BG Guam May 1945. *NASM*

Biscay Belle B-24 479 Anti-submarine GP 8 AF *NASM*

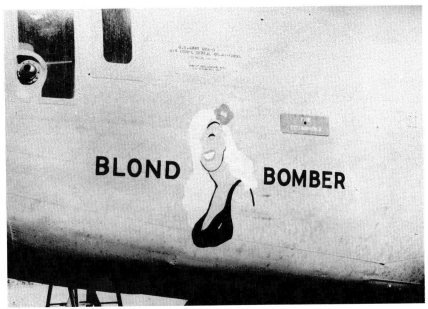

Blond Bomber B-24 41-11095 NASM

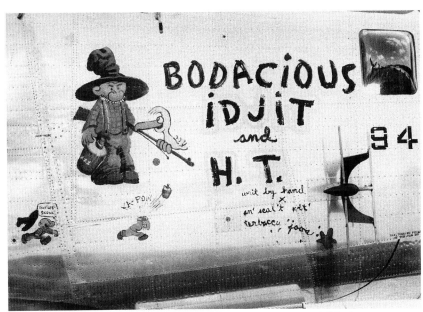

Bodacious Idjit and H.T. B-24 11 BG Guam May 1945. Caption "Writ By Hand X an' Seal't Wit' Terbaccu Joos." NASM

Bomb Babe B-24 NASM

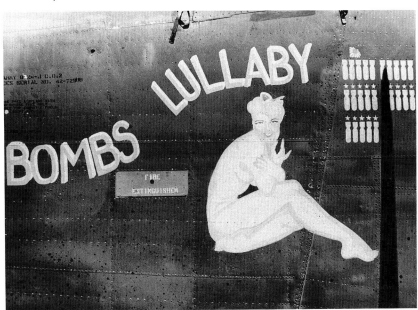

Bombs Lullaby B-24 42-72988 Play on "Brahm's Lullaby." NASM

Bomberang B-24-D 41-29722 8 AF Pronounced "Bomber-Rang." NASM

"Briney Marlin" B-24 458 BG 8 AF Lt. Lester C. Marlin with his B-24. NASM

Bugs Buggy B-24 NASM

The Bull B-24 NASM

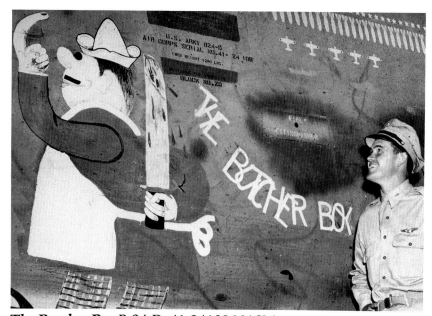

The Butcher Boy B-24-D 41-24108 NASM

Heaven Can Wait B-24 NASM

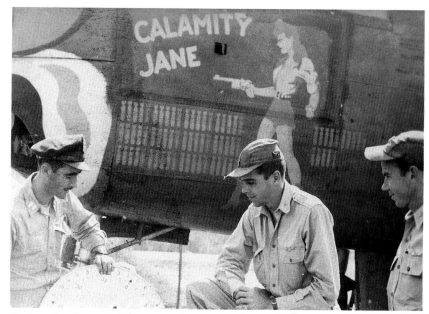

Calamity Jane B-25 Somewhere in India. NASM

Celhalopdos B-24 A slight misspelling of "Cephalopoda" of which the octopus is a member. NASM

Contrary Mary! B-24 NASM

Crash Kids B-24 NASM

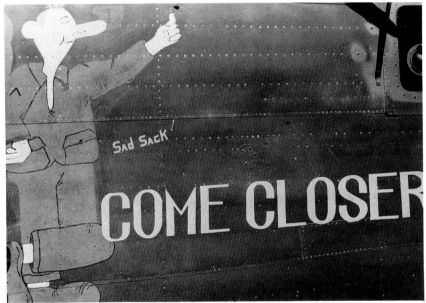

Come Closer B-24 Photo taken in Saipan. NASM

Cowbird B-24 NASM

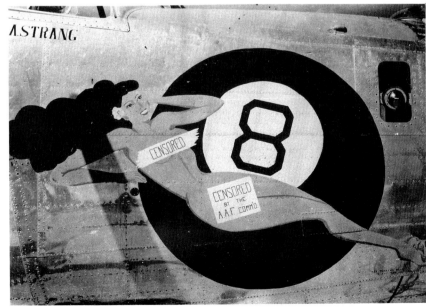

Censored nose art on a B-24 NASM

Darlin Dutchess & the 10 Dukes B-24 42-64500 NASM

Don't Cry Baby B-24 8 AF Photo taken after a nose wheel failure and crash landing near Charling, England. *NASM*

Double Trouble B-24 *NASM*

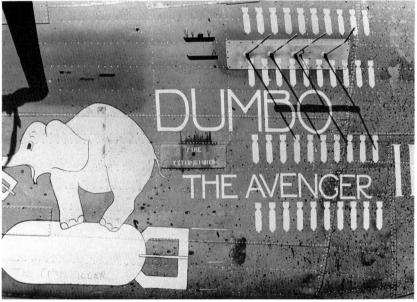

Dumbo II—The Avenger B-24 Kwajalein July 1944. Note that someone has scratched "The Fish Killer" on the bomb—a comment on their bombing accuracy? *NASM*

El Lobo B-24 *NASM*

V-Grand 5000 B-24 The 5000th B-24 built—signed by the factory workers—also see B-17 ***5-Grand.*** *NASM*

The Flying Fifer B-24 *NASM*

Fools Paradise B-24-J 42-73282 Kwajalein July 1944. NASM

Frenisi B-24 Pronounced "Free n Easy." The crew and aircraft after the 100th mission. NASM

Gas House Mouse B-24-H 753 BS 458 BG 8 AF NASM

Ginny Lynn B-24 Photo taken on Nanumea Island NASM

Glenna Bee II B-24 Kwajalein July 1944. NASM

Hell's Belle B-24 704 BS 446 BG 8 AF NASM

Hit-Parade B-24 NASM

Innocence A-Broad B-24 NASM

Kansas Cyclone B-24 26 BS 11 BG NASM

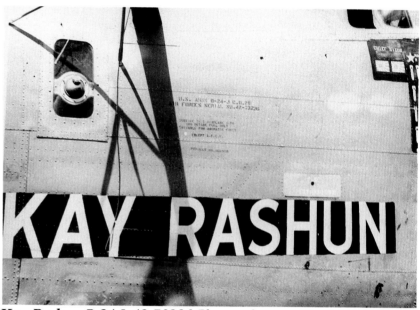

Kay Rashun B-24-J 42-70236 Photo taken on Kwajalein July 1944. Named after the GI's 2nd favorite meal (after Spam). NASM

"Kickapoo-Kid" B-24-J 42-72003 Kwajalein July 1944. NASM

Lucky Dog B-24 11 BG Guam May 1945. NASM

Lady Leone B-24 NASM

Late Date B-24 NASM

"Lakanooki" B-24-D 41-24810 Pronounced "Lack A Nooki." NASM

Lil Audrey B-24-J 42-79416 Aircraft completed 100 missions in the Marianas. NASM

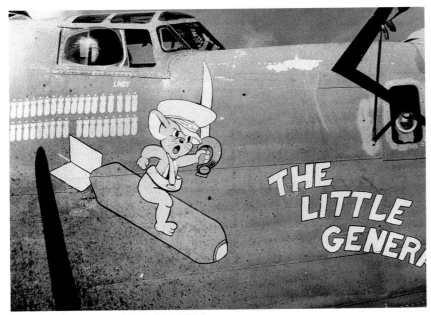

The Little General B-24 NASM

Little Hiawatha B-24 Funafuti, Ellice Island. Gen. Hale and B-24 crew with a bomb autographed by Bing Crosby. NASM

Little Red B-24 NASM

Lizzy Belle B-24 490 BG 8 AF NASM

Mad Russian B-24 NASM

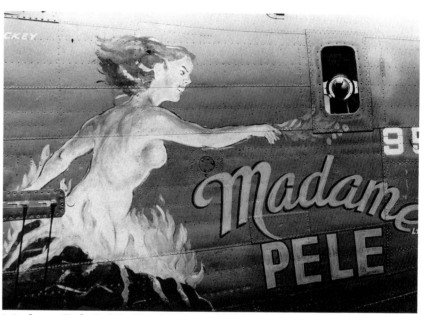

Madame Pele B-24 42-109951 26 BS 11 BG 7 AF Purchased with funds raised by Hawaiian school children and named for the Hawaiian goddess of fire. NASM

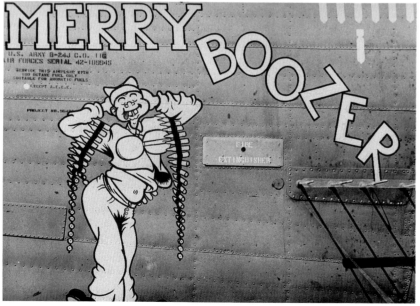

Merry Boozer B-24-J 42-109945 Kwajalein July 1944. NASM

Michigan B-24-J-161-CO 44-40429 43 BG NASM

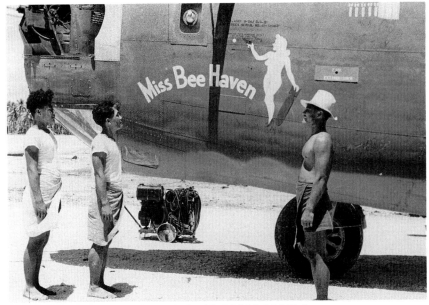

Miss Bee Haven B-24-J-CO-2 42-72982 *NASM*

The Missouri Mule B-24 494 BG Col. Kelly of the 494th stands besides the wrecked B-24 April 10, 1945, Angaur Island *NASM*

Murphy's Mother In Law B-24 Worse than Murphy's Law (if anything can go wrong—it will). *NASM*

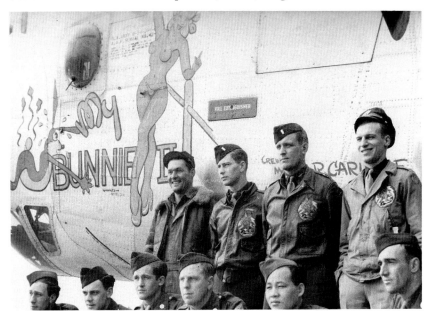

My Bunnie II B-24 8 AF *NASM*

My Diversion B-24 *NASM*

Near Miss B-24 *NASM*

Nipponese Clipper B-24 38 BS 30 BG *NASM*

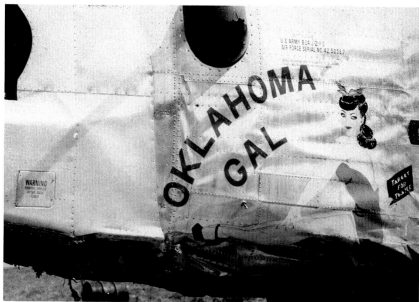

Oklahoma Gal B-24-J 42-50567 8 AF Slight undercarriage damage after crash landing at Bungay, Norfolk, England, August 27, 1944. *NASM*

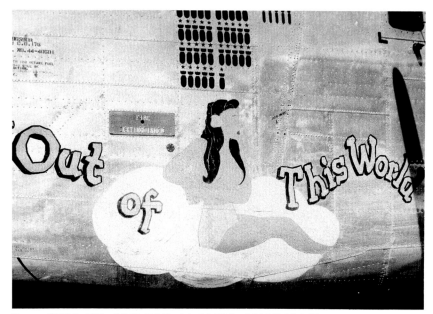

Out of This World B-24-J 44-40601 11 BG *NASM*

Photo Queen B-24 Photo recon. *NASM*

Pistol Pakin Mamma B-24 Kwajalein 1944. *NASM*

Play Boy B-24 *NASM*

Pleasure Bent B-24 AFM

Plunderbus B-24 NASM

Rose of Juarez B-24 8 AF NASM

Riot Call B-24 NASM

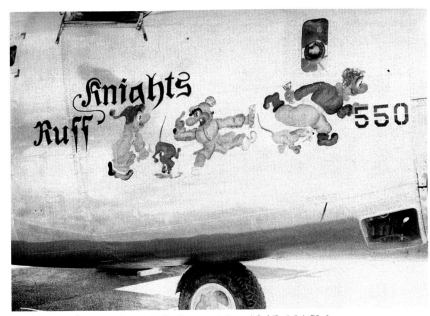

Ruff Knights B-24 11 BG Guam May 1945. NASM

Ruthless Ruthie B-24 8 AF Note armor plate add-on over nose art. NASM

Sack Time Sal II B-24 NASM

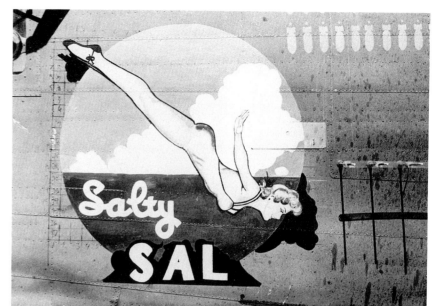

Salty Sal B-24 Kwajalein July 1944. NASM

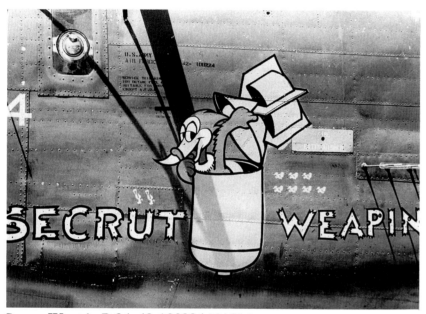

Secrut Weapin B-24 42-100224 NASM

Shady Lady B-24-J 8 AF Wrecked November 27, 1944. NASM

Smokey Stover B-24 NASM

Snootie Cutie B-24 490 BG 8 AF Lt. Holden and crew. NASM

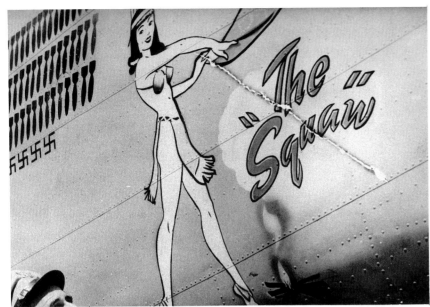

The Squaw B-24 8 AF Crewman inspects flak damage. *NASM*

"Tail Winds" B-24 8 AF *NASM*

Tarfu B-24 42-109933 Kwajalein. Pronounced "Things are Really Fouled Up." *NASM*

Temptation B-24-I 44-40617 *NASM*

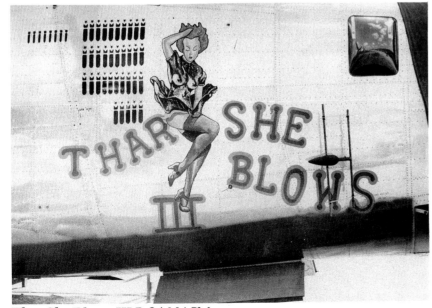

Thar She Blows III B-24 *NASM*

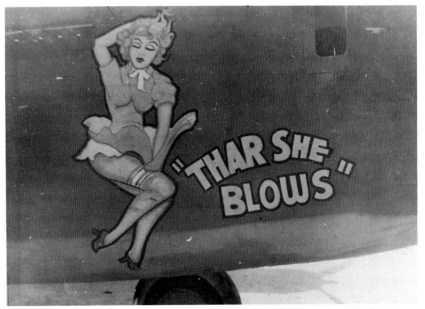

Thar She Blows B-24-D 42 BS 11 BG July 1943 Kualoa, Oahu. *Albert Marston*

Tropical Trollop B-24 NASM

12 Targets to Tokyo B-24 NASM

Umbriago! B-24 NASM

Virgin Vampire B-24 Note prop damage. NASM

The Vulgar Virgin B-24 41-24192 NASM

USAFI B-24 8 AF NASM

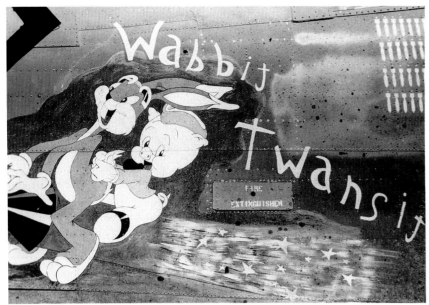

Wabbit Twansit B-24 Kwajalein July 1944. *NASM*

Wild Ass Ride B-24 11 BG Guam May 1945. *NASM*

Wolf B-25 *NASM*

"Wolf-Pack" B-25 43 BG February 1944 Papua-New Guinea. *NASM*

Worth Fighting For B-24 *NASM*

You Bet! B-24 *NASM*

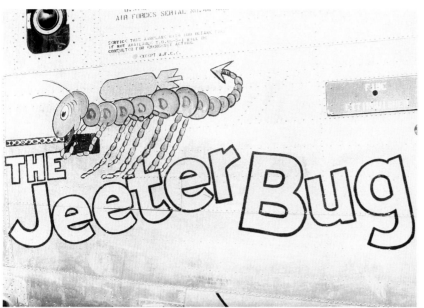

The Jeeter Bug B-24-J 44-40661 Marianas Island. *NASM*

B-24 *NASM*

B-24 *NASM*

B-24 *NASM*

B-24 42-109838 *NASM*

B-24 *NASM*

148

B-24 Nose art in progress, note photo taped to plane. *NASM*

B-24 Crew stands for 100th mission photo. *NASM*

B-24 *NASM*

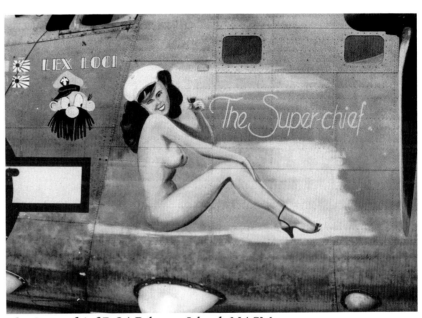

The Superchief B-24 Palawan Island. *NASM*

"This Above All" B-24 *NASM*

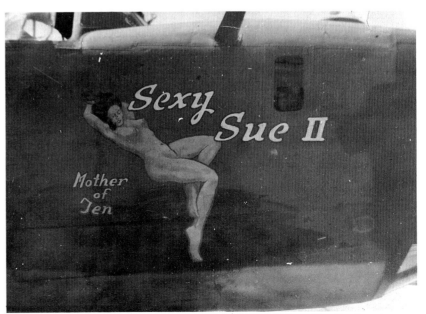

Sexy Sue II B-24-D 41-23925 98 BS 11 BG Piloted by Lt. Lewis Cartwright, crash landed on Makin Island, after a mission in the Marshalls, December 18, 1943. *A. Marston*

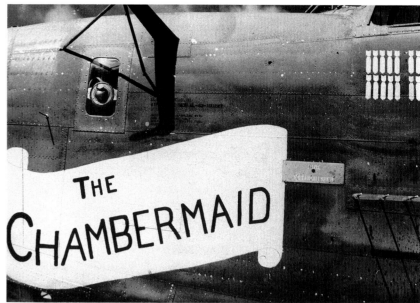

Dogpatch Express B-24-D 41-24214 Crew and plane lost December 20, 1943, over Maloelap Atoll. *A. Marston*

The Chambermaid B-24 NASM

The Pelican B-24 NASM

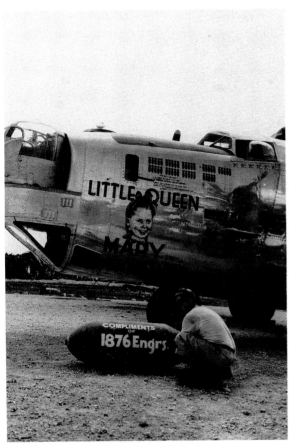

Little Queen Mary B-24 NASM

Big Chief Cockeye B-24 Note: hold the photo close up and far away. AFM

Black Magic B-24 7 BG 9 BS 10 AF L. Huken

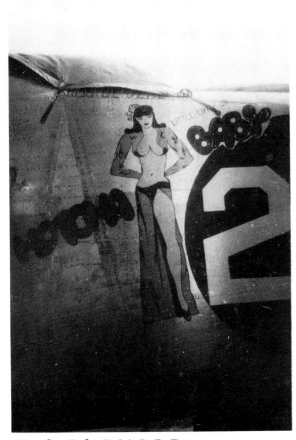

Hotcha Baby B-24 C. P. Dicecco

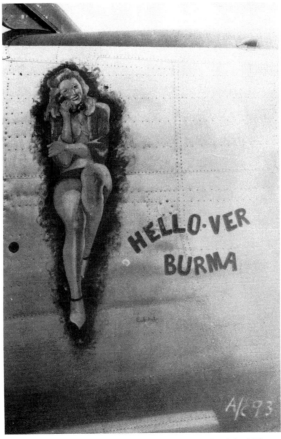

Hello-ver Burma B-24 7 BG 9 BS 10 AF L. Huken

Mask-A-Raid B-24 W. Hughs

151

Nocturnal Mission B-24 AFM

Over Exposed B-24 Photo recon. AFM

Peace Offering B-24 43 BG 403 BS AFM

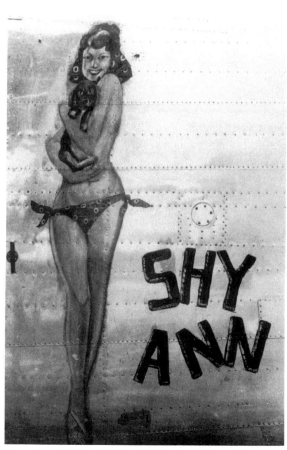

Rose O' Day B-24 AFM

Rangy Lil B-24

Shy Ann B-24 7 BG 9 BS 10 AF *L. Huken*

Wonderous Wanda B-24 44-40562 AFM

B-24 C. P. Dicecco

B-24 Vargas-inspired nose art. C. P. Dicecco

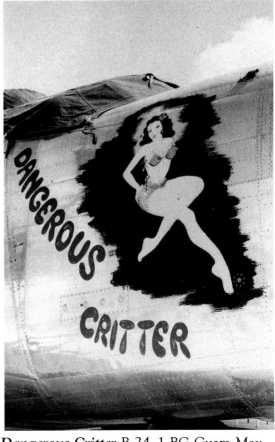

Brunnhilda B-24 Mechanics repair flak damage on Funafuti, Ellice Island November 17, 1943. *NASM*

B-24 Original name not known, but it offended someone. Note flak damage. *NASM*

Dangerous Critter B-24 1 BG Guam May 1945. *NASM*

Feather Merchants B-24 NASM

Going My Way B-24-J 11 BG Guam May 1944. NASM

Miss Traveler B-24 11 BG Guam May 1945. Note trunk stickers: Tokyo-Guam-Kwajalein-Tinian-Siapan. NASM

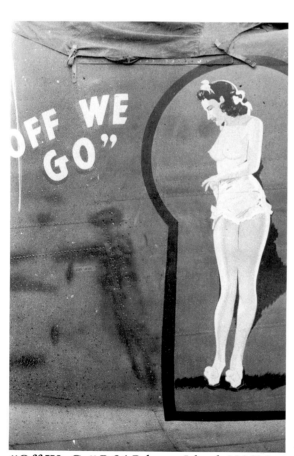

"Off We Go" B-24 Palawan Island. NASM

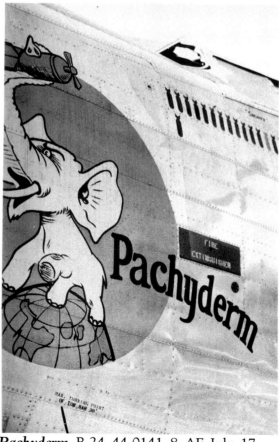

Pachyderm B-24 44-0141 8 AF July 17, 1944. NASM

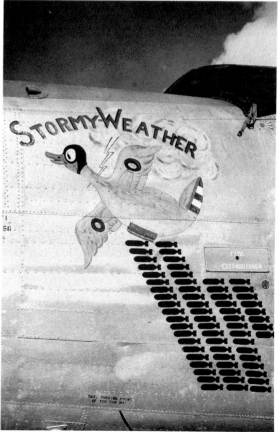

Stormy Weather B-24 44-40556 11 BG Guam May 1945. NASM

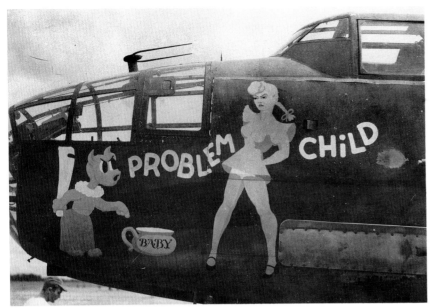

Problem Child B-25 82BS 12BG *John Lawler*

Our Gal Ardelle B-25 82 BS 12 BG *J. Lawler*

Leroy's Joy B-25 82 BS 12 BG *CBI Theater. NASM*

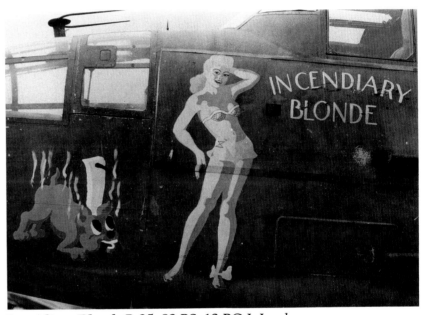

Incendiary Blonde B-25 82 BS 12 BG *J. Lawler*

Bam's Mam B-25 82 BS 12 BG *J. Lawler*

Prop Wash B-25 82 BS 12 BG *J. Lawler*

Calcutta Commando B-25 82 BS 12 BG Note: per diem (per day) is an extra allowance given to those on temporary duty away from their normal duty station. *J. Lawler*

Miss-Behav' in B-25 82 BS 12 BG *J. Lawler*

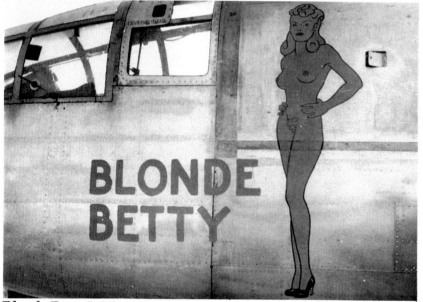

Blonde Betty B-25 82 BS 12 BG *J. Lawler*

Vikin's Vicious Virgin B-25 82 BNS 12 BG *J. Lawler*

The Black Widow B-25 82 BS 12 BG *J. Lawler*

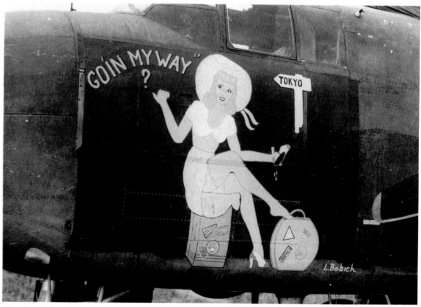

Go'in My Way? B-25 82 BS 12 BG *J. Lawler*

Sal B-25 82 BS 12 BG Note the paint removed by the muzzle blast of the 50-cal. machine gun. *J. Lawler*

The First Mistake B-25 AFM

Desert Warrior B-25 9 AF Note map with missions. *NASM*

Bones B-25 81 BS 12 AF Covered with names of employees of the North American aviation production plant. *NASM*

Frisky Frisco B-25 *NASM*

"Gorgeous Georgetta" B-25 81 BS 12 BG India. *NASM*

Hardships 2nd B-25 NASM

"*Potch-A-Goloop*" B-25 41-12562 AFM

Pluto B-25 Photo taken somewhere in Africa. NASM

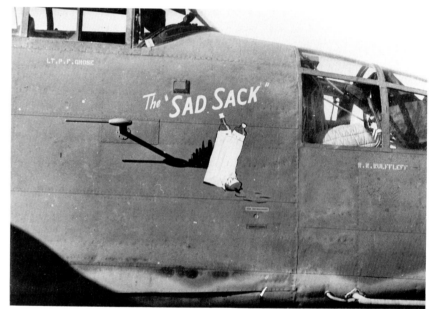

The "Sad Sack" B-25 AFM

Skunk Hunter B-25 AFM

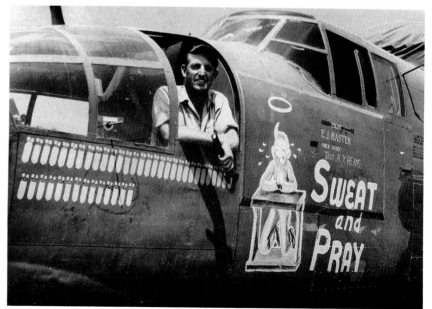

Sweat and Pray B-25 Tsgt. Alex Reams, crew chief, looks out of his aircraft. NASM

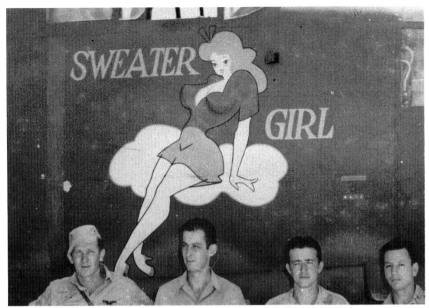

Sweater Girl B-25 18 combat mapping squad. 1943 Espiritu Santo, New Hebrides. NASM

Stud B-25 NASM

Sweet Lorraine B-25 81 BS 12 BG NASM

Texas Gal B-25 Note late model B-25 with cannon port. NASM

Valiant Virgin! B-25 AFM

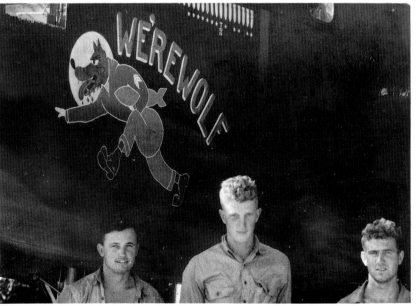

We're Wolf B-25 71 SQ NASM

159

Golden Gate or Bust B-25 NASM

Nose art on one of the B-25s that went on the Doolittle Raid on Tokyo. *NASM*

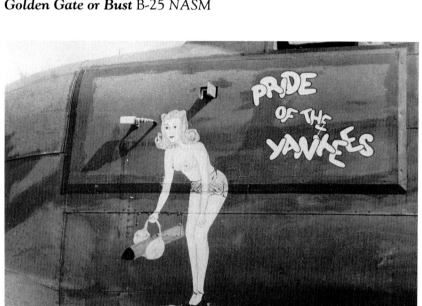

Pride of the Yankees B-25 820 BS 41 BG *NASM*

Bitemontheas' B-25 AFM

B-25 NASM

Ou-La-La A-20 NASM

Jivin' Julie B-25 82 BS 12 BG J. Lawler

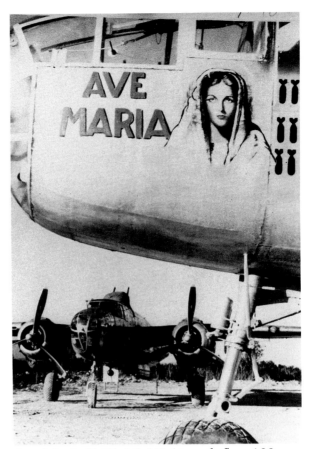

Ave Maria B-25 12 AF Aircraft flew 103 missions. *NASM*

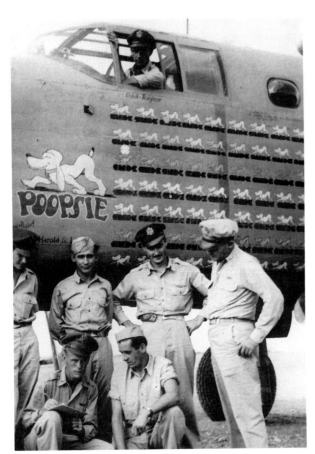

Poopsie B-25 There are 66 little Poopsies on the aircraft, and 4 of the crew have 50 missions. *NASM*

The Marlin B-26 NASM

The Chief B-26 NASM

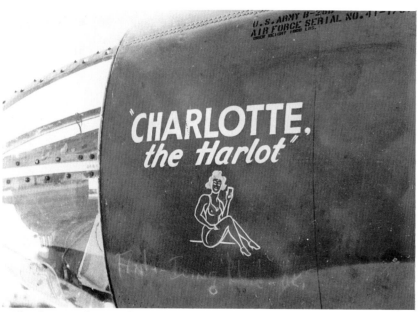

"Charlotte, The Harlot" B-26 41-17818 AFM

Flak Bait B-26-B 41-31773 449 BS 322 BG Flew 202 missions; now in National Air and Space Museum, NASM

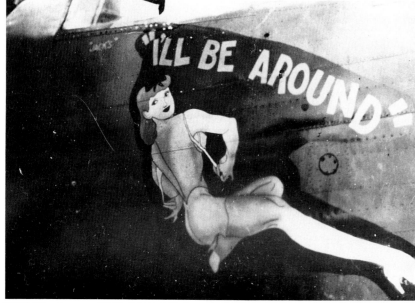

"I'll Be Around" B-26 NASM

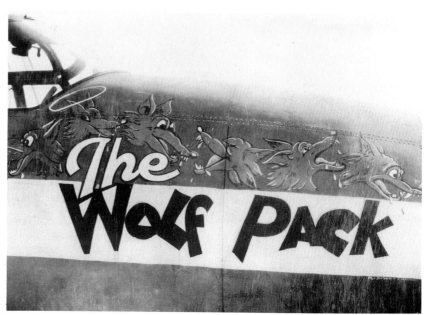

The Wolf Pack B-26 AFM

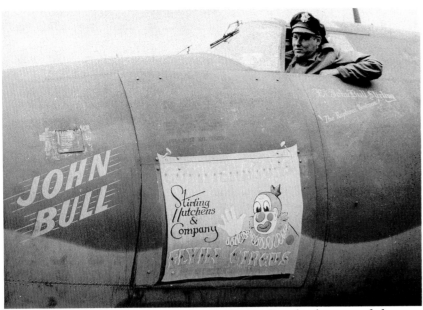

John Bull B-26 8 AF Lt. "John Bull" Stirling looks out of the pilot's window of his B-26. *NASM*

John Bull B-26 8 AF *NASM*

The Mad Russian B-26 381 BG 555 BS 8 AF *NASM*

Murder Inc B-26 41-18272 322 BG 8 AF Shot down, and crew captured wearing their A-2 jackets with "Murder Inc" on the back. The Germans made a propaganda film of the "Murderers" that was widely shown in Europe. After this incident, there was a review of all nose art names. *NASM*

Old Crow *NASM*

Our Baby B-26 353 BS 386 BG 8 AF *NASM*

Rationed Passion B-26 391 BG 8 AF *NASM*

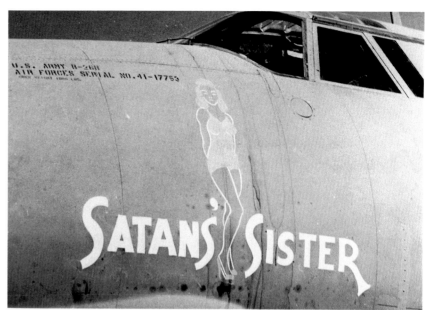

Satan's Sister B-26 41-17753 *AFM*

The Swoose B-26 *NASM*

Texas Peace Maker B-26 *NASM*

Tootsie B-26 *NASM*

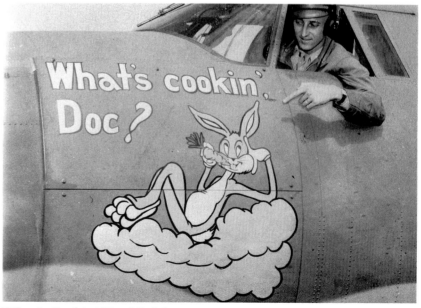

What's Cookin' Doc? B-26 8 AF *NASM*

B-26 41-34894 NASM

Zombie II B-26 NASM

"Little Gal" B-26 AFM

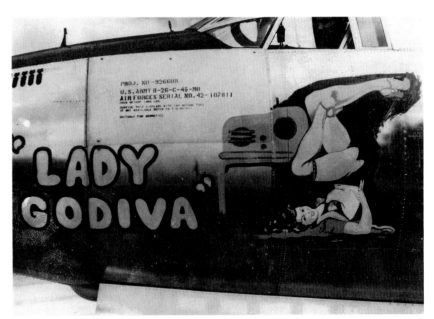

"Lady Godiva" B-26-C 42-107811 AFM

Purrin' Panther B-26 AFM

Maytag Marauder B-26 AFM

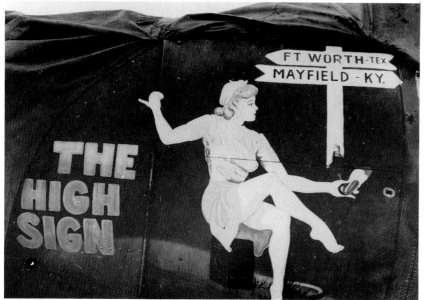

The High Sign B-26 AFM

Lady Chance B-26 NASM

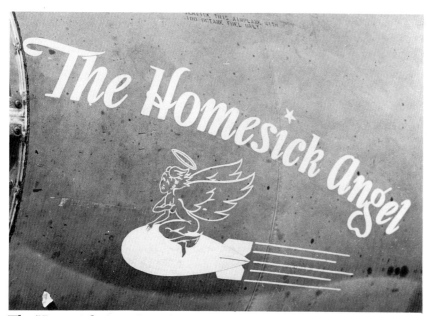

The Homesick Angel B-26 41-17760 AFM

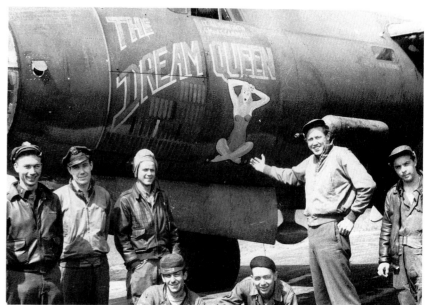

The Dream Queen B-26 AFM

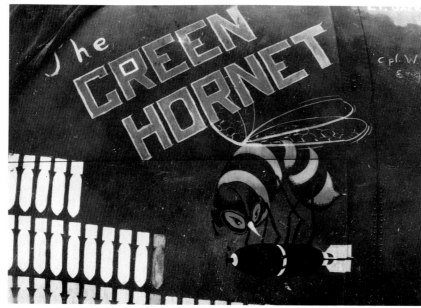

The Green Hornet B-26 AFM

"Scorpion" B-26 AFM

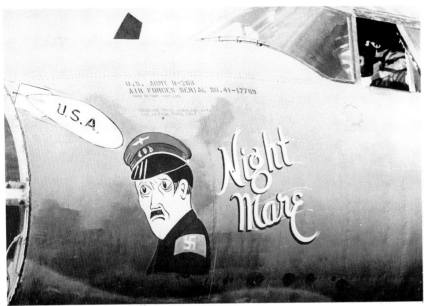

Night Mare B-26-B 41-17769 AFM

Geronimo B-26 AFM

Sky Hag B-26 575 BS 391 BG 8 AF AFM

T.S. B-26 AFM

Hell's Belle II B-26 AFM

"Miss Laid" B-26 AFM

Rum Buggy B-26 NASM

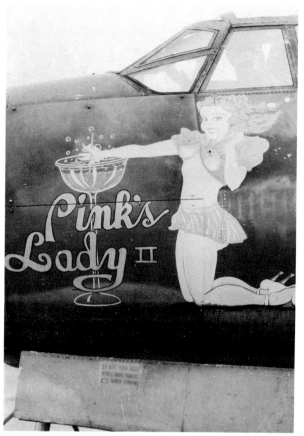

Pink's Lady II B-26 391 BG 8 AF NASM

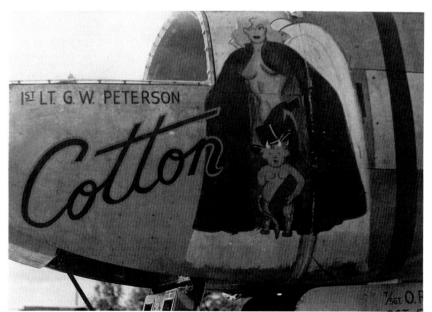

Cotton A-26-C 386 BG 9 AF T. Bivens

Kiwi Boid A-26-B 43-22410 386 BG 9 AF T. Bivens

Skonk Works A-20 AFM

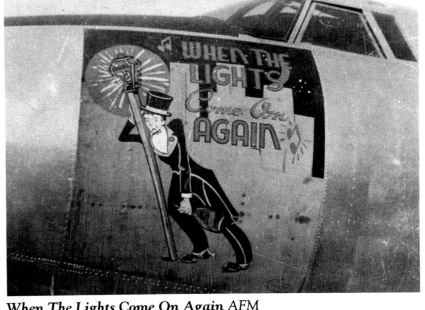

When The Lights Come On Again AFM

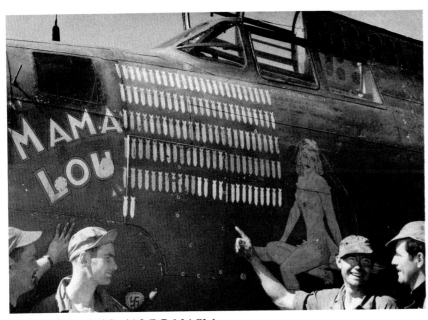

Mama Lou A-20 410 BG NASM

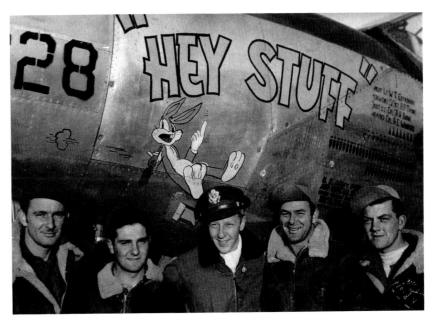

"Hey Stuff" P-38 367 FTR GP 8AF NASM

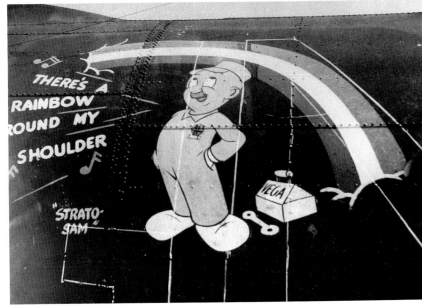

There's a Rainbow Round My Shoulder AFM

Double Busted Toby From Muskogee A-20 NASM

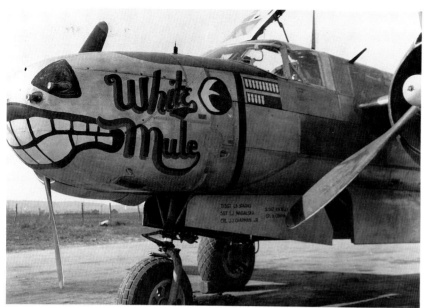

White Mule A-26B 386 BG 9 AF Beaumont, France 1944. *T. Bivens*

Bambi P-38 *NASM*

Big Stud P-47 *AFM*

Camera Shy P-38. Photo recon. *AFM*

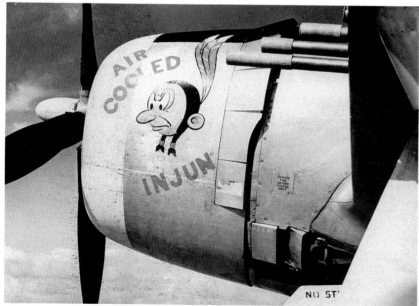

Air Cooled Injun P-47 Is the engine or the Injun air cooled? *NASM*

Arkansas Traveler P-38 367 Fighter GP Lt. Lincher sits in the cockpit of his P-38. *AFM*

The wreck of the P-47 **Big Bastard** in Iceland. NASM

Litle Buckaroo P-38 367 FTR GP NASM

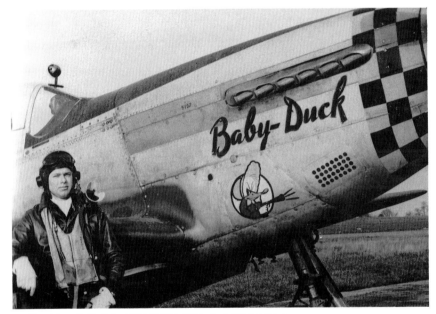

Baby-Duck P-51 353 FTR GP 8 AF NASM

Cold Feet A-20 410 BG NASM

Eloise A-20 Real "nose" art. NASM

In Memory of Lt. F. Slanger U.S.A.N.C. P-38 367 FTR GP
December 1944. AFM

Mary Lou AFM

Minnehaha P-51 44-11152 Lt. Shilt of the 353rd FTR GP. NASM

Miss Fire P-47 NASM

Miss Mass P-38 367 FTR GP Note umbrellas for top cover missions. NASM

Posse P-38-J Note the train kills, hats, umbrellas and brooms. NASM

"Philbert" 3 P-38 367 FTR GP NASM

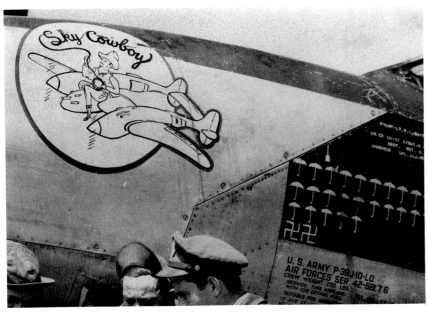

Sky Cowboy P-38-J 42-68176 AFM

Little Chief AFM

P-40 Warhawks *NASM*

P-40 Warhawks *AFM*

L-5 Recon aircraft. Some of the best artwork was on the smallest airplanes. *AFM*

Sweet Revenge 8 AF AFM

San Antonio Rose NASM

Dottie Anne NASM

The Goose C-47 NASM

The Swoose—It flys NASM

"The Gremlin" NASM

Dream Girl C-47 NASM

Times-A-Wastin A-20 NASM

Hell's Belle P-47 AFM

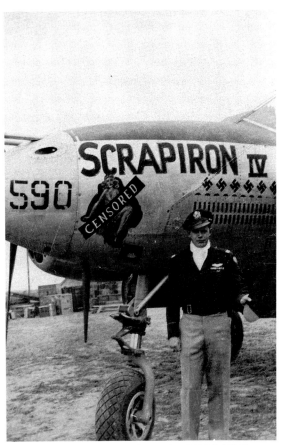

Scrapiron IV P-38 367 FTR GP NASM

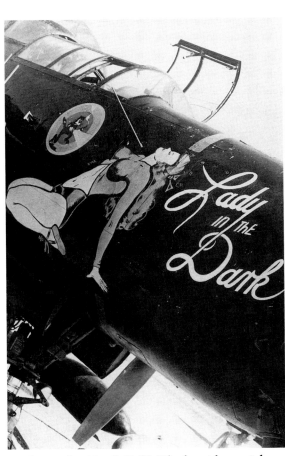

Lady in the Dark P-61 Black widow night fighter AFM

Reading the "Woonsocket Call" under an *Esquire*/Vargas calendar is Johnny Godfrey, 36 kill ace of the 4th Fighter Group. *Esquire.* AFM

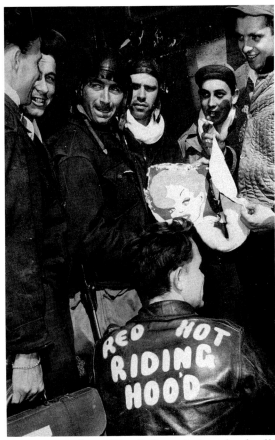

Red Hot Riding Hood Crew brings back all that is left of their bomber after a crash landing. NASM

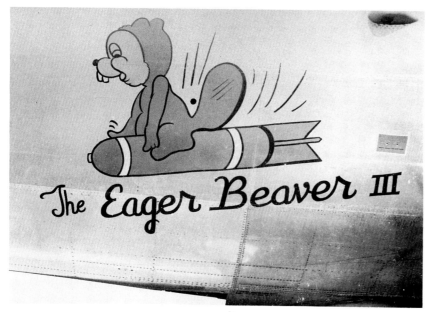

The Eager Beaver III B-29 AFM

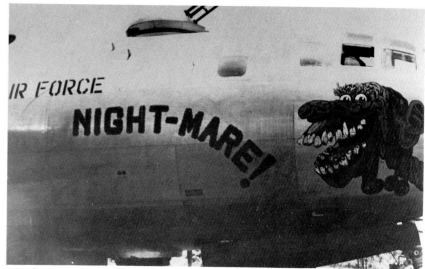

Night Mare B-29 44-87661 28 BS 19 BG Also called "Ugly" and "The Koza Kid." The B-29 was named "Ugly" when it moved to a new base near the village of Koza. When the crew laid eyes on the local cuties, they renamed the plane "The Koza Kid." This upset the local powers, and the plane was renamed again. *AFM*

Rock Happy B-29 AFM

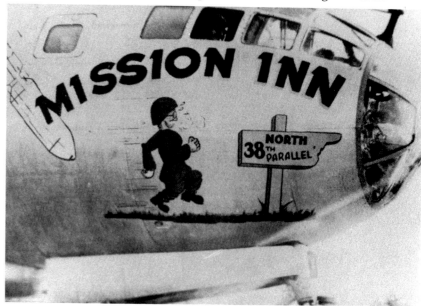

Mission Inn B-29 22BG and 19 BG R. Mann

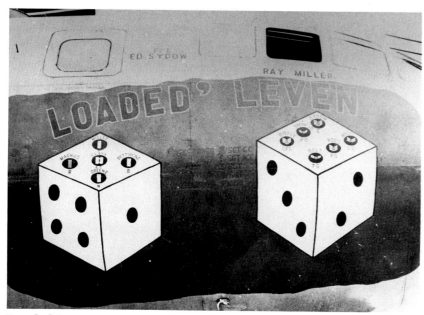

Loaded Leven B-29 Note crew names on the dice. AFM

Thunderhead B-29 AFM

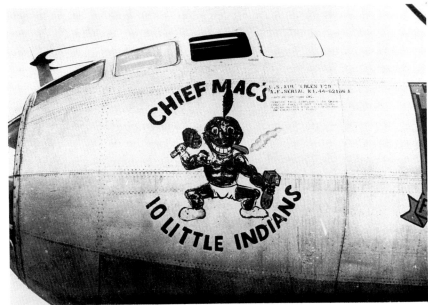

Chief Mac's 10 Little Indians B-29 44-62186 AFM

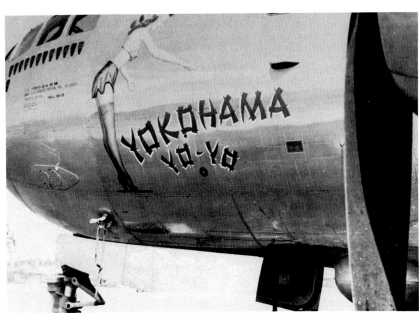

Yokohama Yo-Yo B-29 42-24621 73BW AFM

Jokers Wild B-29 42-24626 AFM

Nose art in progress AFM

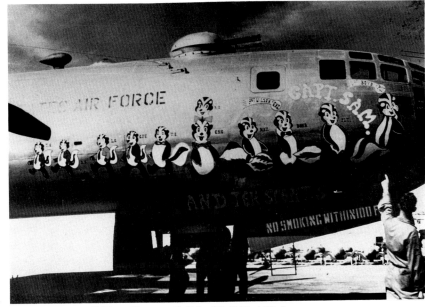

Capt Sam and Ten Scents B-29 19 BG AFM

Phippen's Pippins B-29 AFM

Miss Minooki B-29 AFM

Honshu Hawk B-29 42-64444 AFM

Command Decision B-29 44-87657 19 BG 28 BS One of the most decorated planes of the war. AFM

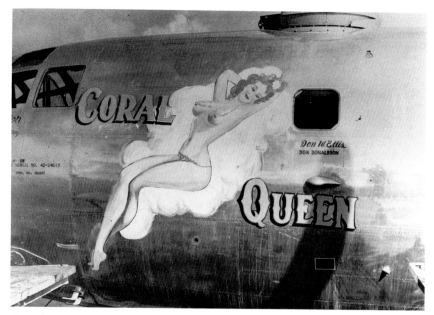

Coral Queen B-29 42-24615 AFM

Antoinette B-29 42-24751 AFM

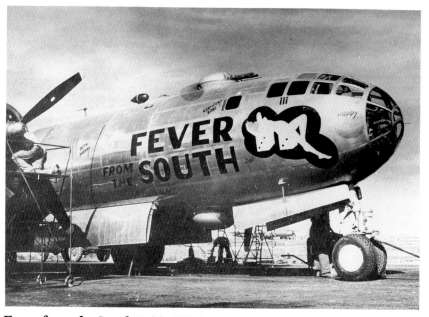

Fever from the South B-29 AFM

Devil's Darlin' B-29 42 24629 TSQ-9 12 AF Lost February 1945. AFM

Long Distance B-29 42-24544 12 AF AFM

Lonely Lady B-29 AFM

Squeeze Play B-29 44-86415 98 BG R. Mann

Dragon Lady B-29 AFM

Destiny's Tots B-29 AFM

179

Waddy's Wagon B-29 42-24598 ASQ-5 12 AF Aircraft and crew lost returning from a raid on Tokyo January 9, 1945. *NASM*

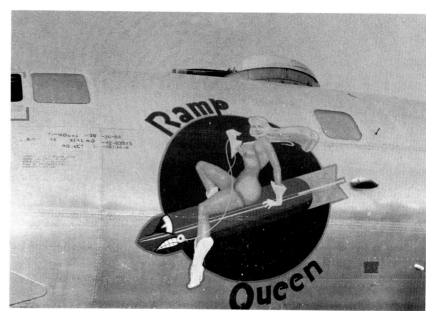

Ramp Queen B-29 42-63513 *AFM*

Tanaka Termite B-29 *AFM*

Passion Wagon B-29 42-63324 *AFM*

Strange Cargo B-29 44-27300 Note the "Fat Man" mission markers (early nuclear bomb tests). *AFM*

Heavenly Body B-29 *AFM*

Myasis Dragon B-29 98 BG 12 AF R. Mann

Our Gal B-29 AFM

Shanghai Lil Rides Again B-29 676 BS AFM

Ogoshi Ni B-29 AFM

20th Century Sweetheart B-29 AFM

Lucky Lady B-29 AFM

"Double Whammy" B-29 19 BG 12 AF NASM

Beaubomber II B-29 AFM

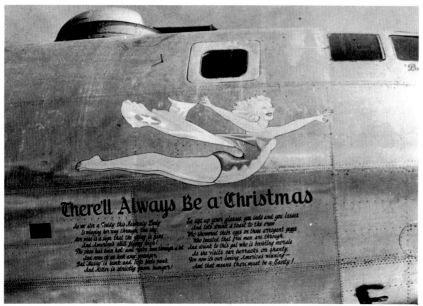

There'll Always Be A Christmas B-29 AFM

Snugglebunny B-29 44-69667 98 BG The original name was on the aircraft during its thirty-five missions in World War II. The artwork was added in Korea where it flew an additional sixty-five combat missions. *R. Mann*

Poison Ivy B-29 AFM

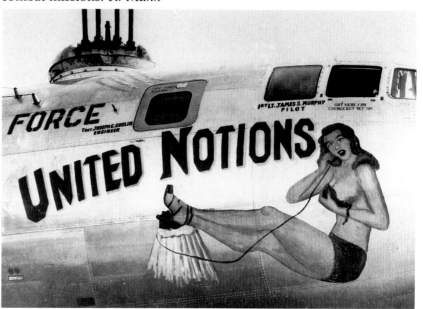

United Notions B-29 98 BG A play on words, United Nations, during the United Nations police action in Korea. *R. Mann*

182

"Deal Me In" B-29 44-96805 98 BG Original name was "Ace in the Hole;" changed by request of the chaplin. *R. Mann*

The Big Gass Bird B-29 98 BW Pronounced "Bigg Ass Bird." AFM

Mrs. Tittymouse B-29 42-65212 NASM

Chicago Sal B-29 AFM

Peace on Earth B-29 42-63412 AFM

Flak Maid B-29 44-70128 AFM

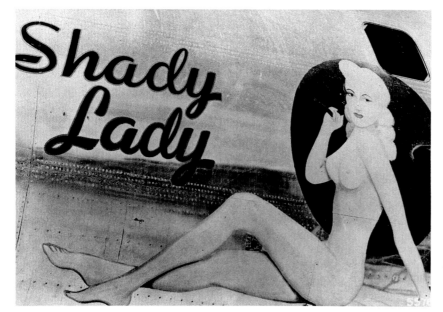

Shady Lady B-29 42-65357 98 BG AFM

Dragon Lady B-29 AFM

The Dragon Lady B-29 AFM

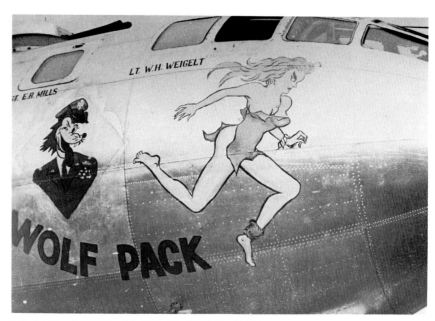

Wolf Pack B-29 44-86340 98 BG AFM

Our Baby B-29 42-24597 AFM

Little Gem B-29 AFM

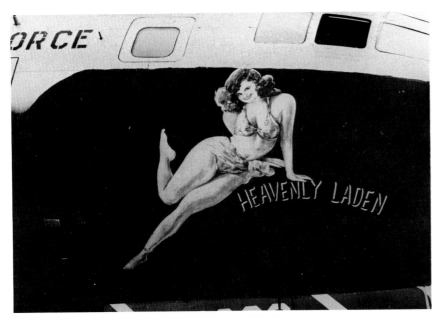

Heavenly Laden B-29 44-61822 98 BG R. Mann

Cream of the Crop B-29 44-61657 19 BG 30 BS AFM

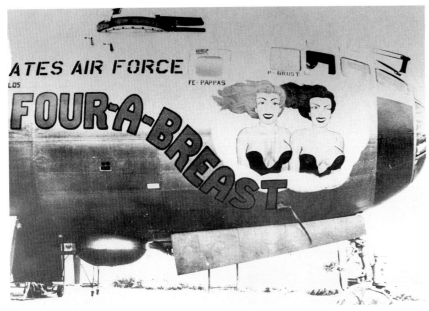

Four-A-Breast B-29 44-86323 19 BG 28 BS AFM

Beetle Bomb Er B-29 44-69800 98 BG Original artwork did not have the girl and was the "Beetle Bomb." AFM

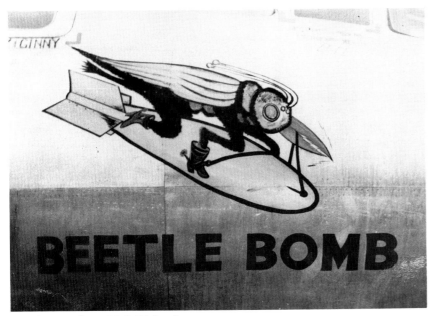

Beetle Bomb B-29 J. Kolander

Purple Shaft B-29 AFM

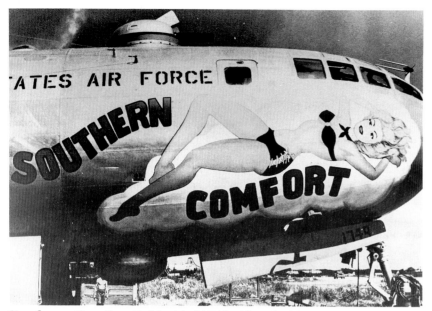

Southern Comfort B-29 44-61749 19 BG 30 BS Lost over Korea November 1950. *AFM*

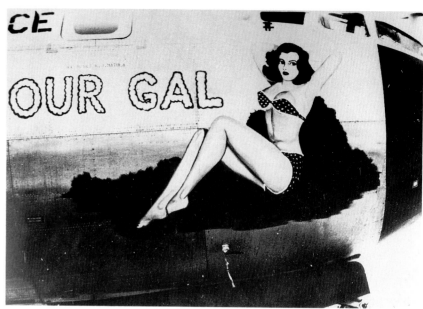

Our Gal B-29 19 BG R. *Mann*

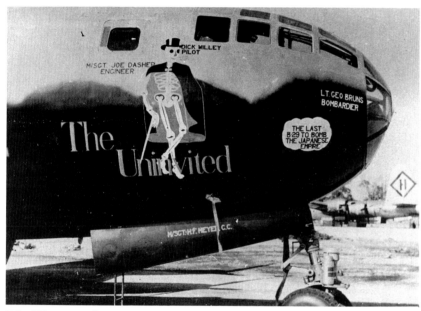

The Uninvited B-29 Note the note. Must have been the last one in line during the last bombing run. *AFM*

The Wanderer B-29 44-62224 94 BG 325 BS Named for Lt. Col. Ralph Wanderer, commander of the 325th BS. So the story goes, Lt. Col. Wanderer was pushing for his full Col.'s bird when it came time to name this aircraft. The aircraft commander, Capt. B. Hemmingway, called it "The Wanderer." A close look reveals that those are not butterflys, but little eagles that he is chasing. *AFM*

Atomic Tom B-29 19 BG 93 BS *AFM*

Miss Megook B-29 "Gook" is slang for a Korean. *AFM*

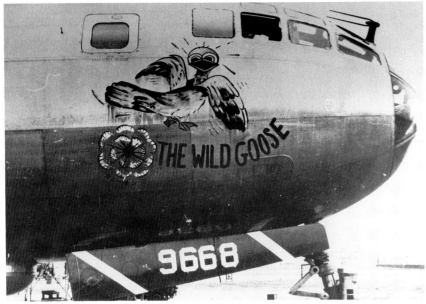

The Wild Goose B-29 AFM

Loaded Dice B-29 AFM

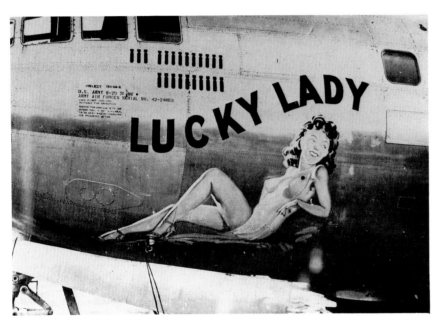

Lucky Lady B-29 42-44863 AFM

Fire Belle B-29 AFM

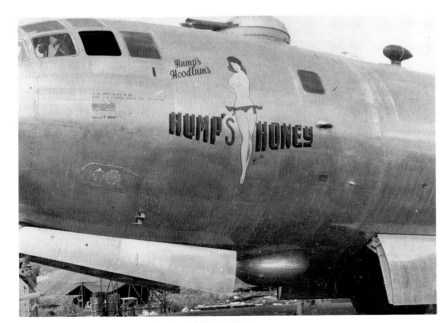

Hump's Honey B-29 42-24648 AFM

Victory Girl B-29 42-24731 AFM

Sentimental Journey B-29 AFM

The Big Stick B-29 42-24661 AFM

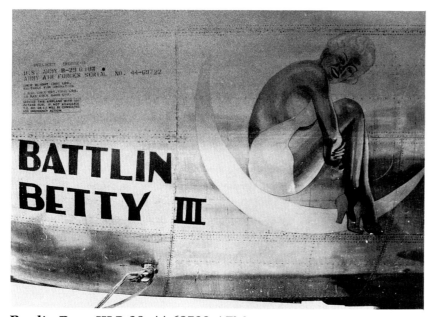

Battlin Betty III B-29 44-69722 AFM

Bedroom Eyes B-29 AFM

Were Wolf B-29 AFM

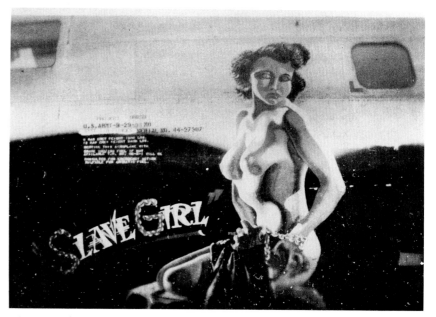

Slave Girl B-29 44-27387 AFM

Nip-Pon-Ese B-29 44-87760 98 BG 93 BS Could be "Nip on Knees" or "Nip on These." AFM

B-29 42-63481 Vargas artwork. AFM

Little Jo B-29 AFM

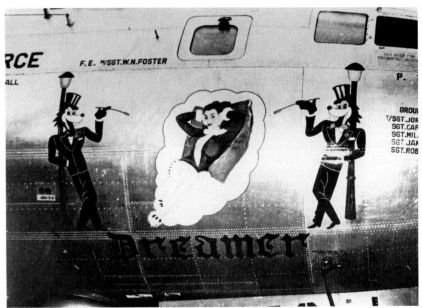

Dreamer B-29 44-87341 98 BG AFM

Dreamer B-29 J. Kolander

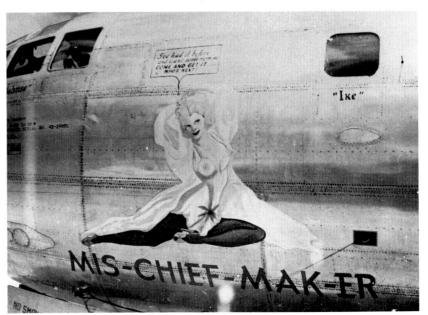

Mis-Chief-Mak-Er B-29 The girl is saying "I've had it before and want some more so come and get it. . . . Whos next!" AFM

189

Lake Success Express B-29 44-69980 98 BG AFM

The Angellic Pig B-29 44-61991 AFM

Big Stink B-29 NASM

Bad Penny B-29 NASM

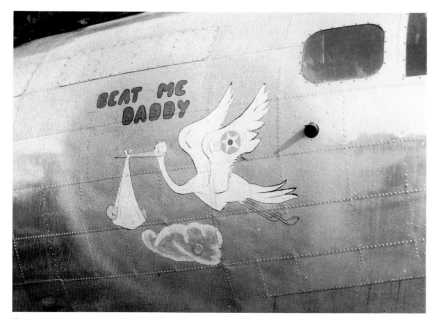

Beat Me Daddy B-29 NASM Quote from the song, "Beat Me Daddy, Eight to the Bar." *NASM*

Black Magic B-29 NASM

The Fat Cat B-29 Note that the mission markers are cows. *NASM*

Devils' Delight B-29 *NASM*

Flying Parts B-29 *NASM*

Fujigmo B-29 *NASM*

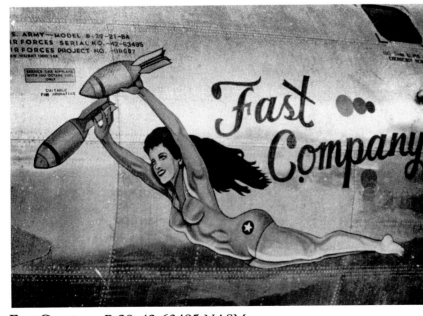

Fast Company B-29 42-63495 *NASM*

The Great Artiste B-29 Flew recon on both atomic bomb drops on Japan, and was later used in atomic bomb testing. Note the "Fat Man" logos. *NASM*

191

Good Humpin' B-29 Seventy-eight camels tell the story of seventy-eight trips "over the hump of the world" (flying over the Himalayas) from India to China. *NASM*

Hump Happy Mammy B-29 *NASM*

Katie B-29 Note the rather crude facilities for the maintenance crews to do their best. *NASM*

Lady Luck B-17 *NASM*

"Laggin Dragon" B-29 *NASM*

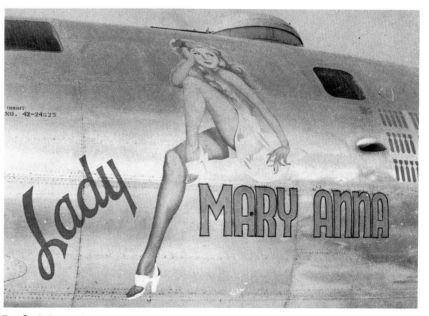

Lady Mary Anna B-29 42-24625 TSQ 12 AF *NASM*

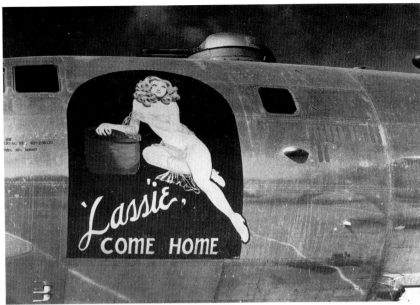

"Lassie", Come Home B-29 42-24609 NASM

Time's A Wastin/Lassie Too! B-29 NASM

Miss Patches B-29 NASM

Marianna Ram B-29 44-69732 AFM

Lucky Lady/Miss Shorty B-29 NASM

Miss Lace B-29 42-63554 NASM

Next Objective B-29 NASM

Over Exposed! B-29 AFM

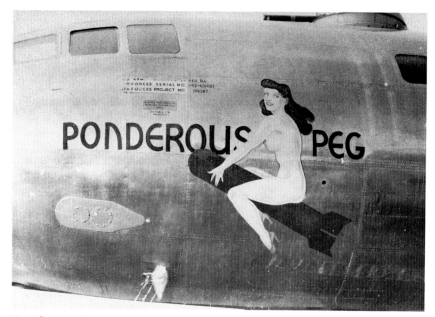

Ponderous Peg B-29 42-63431 AFM

Sheeza Goer! B-29 NASM

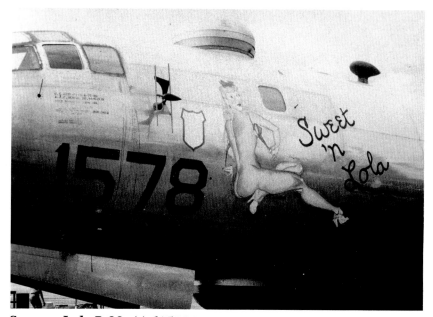

Sweet n Lola B-29 44-61578 NASM

Three Feathers B-29 NASM

Tokyo Rose B-29 Named for the woman in Tokyo who broadcast propaganda messages to GIs during World War II. *NASM*

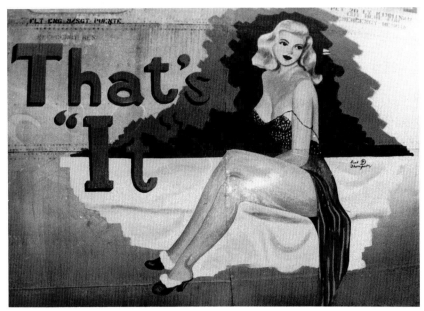

That's "It" B-29 19 BG 93BS *NASM*

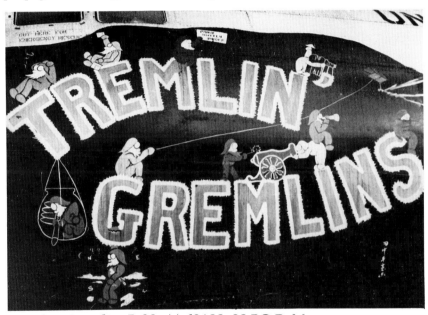

Tremlin' Gremlins B-29 44-62188 98 BG *R. Mann*

Thumper B-29 Note the little thumpers holding flags for fighters shot down. Also the marker bombs have the names of the targets: Truk-Iwo Jima-Tokyo-Tokyo-Nagoya etc. *NASM*

Top Secret B-29 *NASM*

Up An' Atom B-29 44-27304 *NASM*

Princess Eileen II B-29 42-24412 NASM

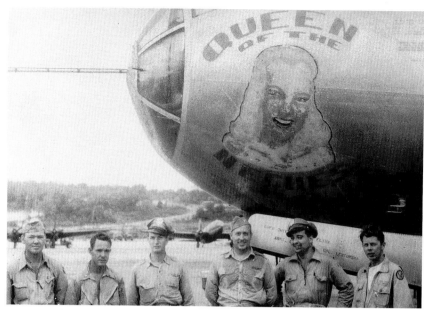

Queen of the Neches B-29 NASM

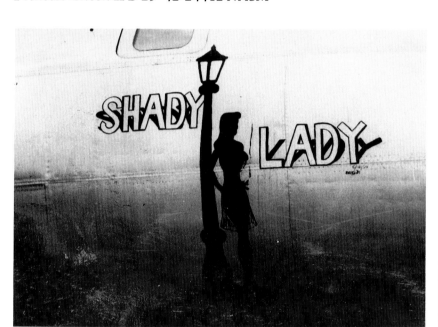

Shady Lady B-29 J. Kolander

T.D.Y Widow B-29 J. Kolander

Winchester "73" Red Raider B-29 98 BG Painted by J. B. Kolander. J. Kolander

196

Snake Bit B-29 J. Kolander

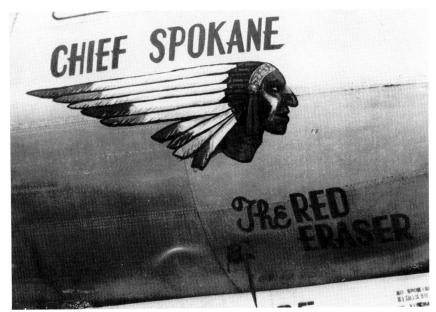

Chief Spokane The Red Eraser B-29. *J. Kolander*

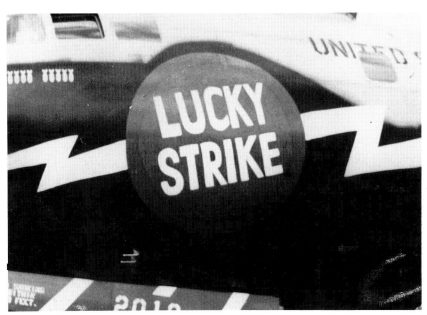

Lucky Strike B-29 44-62070 98 BG *J. Kolander*

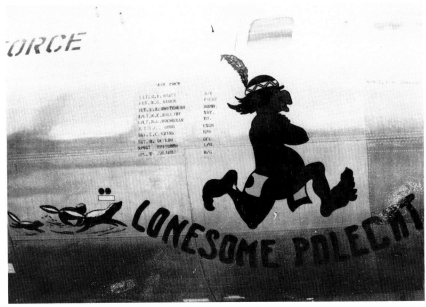

Lonesome Polecat B-29 98 BG *J. Kolander*

Myakinas B-29 44-62108 98 BG *J. Kolander*

Tale of Miss Fortune II B-29 *J. Kolander*

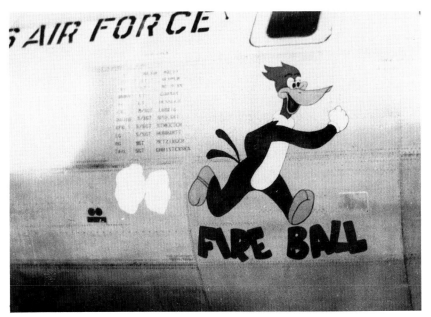

Fire Ball B-29 *J. Kolander*

Tail Wind B-29 J. Kolander

The Worry Bird B-29 Caption reads "Dis Ass Ter." J. Kolander

Liberty Belle B-29 92BG Painted by J. Kolander. J. Kolander

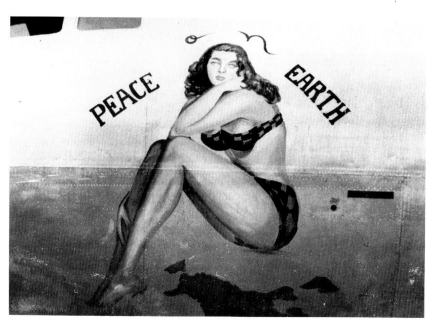

Peace on Earth B-29 J. Kolander

Downs' Clowns B-29 98 BG J. Kolander

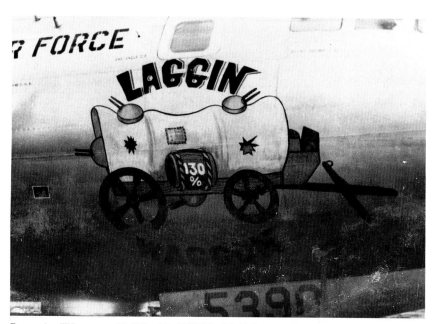

Laggin Waggon B-29 44-65390 98 BG J. Kolander

Texas Doll B-29 AFM

Come on "A" My House B-29 AFM

Southern Belle B-29 42-63478 AFM

Bluetailfly B-29 NASM

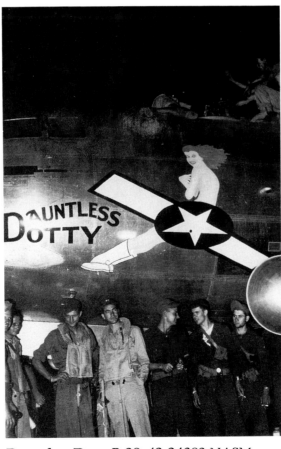

Dauntless Dotty B-29 42-24382 NASM

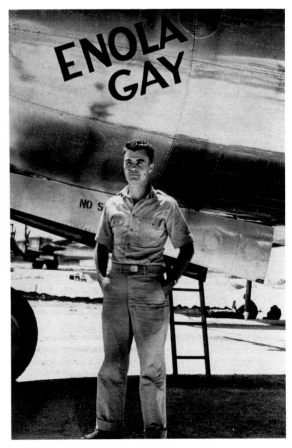

Enola Gay B-29 The pilot, Col. Paul Tibbets, and the plane that dropped the first atomic bomb on (Hiroshima) Japan. The aircaft was named for his mother. Now in the process of restoration at the National Air and Space Museum. NASM

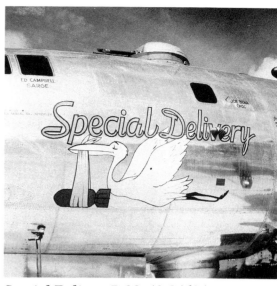

Special Delivery B-29 42-24624 NASM

The Ernie Pyle B-29 44-70118 NASM

Fay B-29 42-65310 NASM

The Wichita Witch B-29 42-24654
NASM

B-29 NASM

B-29 NASM

Index

If the nose art did not have a name, it does not appear in this list. More than one listing for the same name indicates different aircraft. The spelling is as it appears on the aircraft.

NOSE ART NAME	AIRCRAFT TYPE	PAGE NUMBER
Hotcha Baby	B-24	151
"Hot" To Go	B-24	121
Hulcher's Vultures	B-17	54
Hump Happy Mammy	B-29	192
Hump's Honey	B-29	187
Hump Time	B-24	82
Hustlin' Hussy	B-17	39
Ice Cold Katy	B-17	39
Ice Cold Katy	Jacket	75
Ice Col' Katy	B-17	39
Idaliza	B-17	27
Idiots' Delight	B-17	98
I'll Be Around	B-26	162
I'll Be Seeing You	Jacket	75
Impatient Virgin	B-17	62
Impatient Virgin	B-17	62
Incendiary Blonde	B-17	39
Incendiary Blonde	B-25	155
In Memory of Lt. F. Slanger USANC	P-38	171
Innocence A-Broad	B-24	138
Innocent Infant	B-24	121
It Aint So Funny	B-24	121
Iza Vailable Too	B-17	63
Jack the Ripper	B-17	39
Jamaica?	B-24	20
Jap-Happy	B-17	40
Jeeter Bug, The	B-24	148
Jezebel	B-17	40
Jezebelle	B-24	121
Jivin' Julie	B-25	161
John Bull	B-26	163
Joker, The	B-17	40
Joker's Wild, The	B-17	71
Jokers Wild	B-29	177
Jungle Queen	B-24	121
Just Once More	B-17	81
Kansas City Kitty	B-24	122
Kansas Cyclone	B-24	138
Katie	B-29	192
Kay Rashun	B-24	138
Kickapoo-Kid	B-24	138
King's X	B-24	122

NOSE ART NAME	AIRCRAFT TYPE	PAGE NUMBER
Kipling's Error the III	B-17	40
Kiwi Boid	A-26	168
Knock-Out Dropper	B-17	40
Klap-Trap II, The	B-17	40
Kongo Cutie	C-87	122
Lady Chance	B-26	166
Lady Godiva	B-26	165
Lady Helen of Wimpole	B-17	63
Lady in the Dark	P-61	175
Lady Leone	B-24	139
Lady Luck	B-24	85
Lady Luck	B-17	192
Lady Mary Anna	B-29	192
Lady Satan	B-17	41
Laggin Dragon	B-29	192
Laggin Waggon	B-29	198
Lakanooki	B-24	139
Lakanuki	B-17	63
Lake Success Express	B-29	190
"Lassie", Come Home	B-29	193
Lassie I'm Home	B-17	85
Late Date	B-24	139
Lay or Bust	B-17	94
Leo	B-24	90
Leroy's Joy	B-25	155
Lewd Angel	B-17	41
Liberty Belle	B-17	41
Liberty Belle	B-29	198
Libra	B-24	90
Lightning Strikes	B-17	27
Lil Audrey	B-24	139
Lili Marlene	B-24	123
Little Bit "O" Heav'n	B-17	88
Little Buckaroo	P-38	171
Little Cheezer	Jacket	113
Little Chief	?	173
Little Flower	B-24	121
Little Gal	B-26	165
Little Gem	B-29	184
Little General, The	B-24	139
Little Hiawatha	B-24	139
Little Jo	B-29	189
Little Miss Mischief	B-17	99
Little Patches	B-17	63

NOSE ART NAME	AIRCRAFT TYPE	PAGE NUMBER
Little Pedro	B-17	41
Little Pink Panties	B-26	21
Little Queen Mary	B-24	151
Little Red	B-24	140
Little Tush	B-17	41
Lizzy Belle	B-24	140
Loaded Dice	B-29	187
Loaded Leven	B-29	176
Lonely Lady	B-29	179
Lonesome Lady	B-24	122
Lonesome Polecat	B-29	197
Lonesome Polecat Jr	B-24	99
Long Distance	B-29	179
Los Lobos	B-17	41
Lou IV	P-51	101
Lovely Lisa	Jacket	75
Lucky Dog	B-24	138
Lucky Lady	B-29	181
Lucky Lady	B-29	187
Lucky Lady	B-29	193
Lucky Strike	B-29	197
Lucky Strike, The	B-17	63
Lucky Strike	F-111	111
Lucky Strike	B-24	23
Luscious Lace	B-24	122
Madame Pele	B-24	140
Madame Queen	Jacket	79
Madame Queen	B-17	42
Madame Shoo Shoo	B-17	42
Madame-X	B-17	64
Mad Russian	B-24	140
Mad Russian, The	B-26	163
Maggie	B-17	43
Mairzy Doates	B-24	96
Mama Lou	A-20"	169
Mama Foo Foo	B-24	12 & 83
Manchester Misses	B-17	43
Man O War II	B-17	61
Margie	B-17	44
Margie Mae	B-17	42
Marianna Ram	B-29	193
Marlene	B-24	123
Marlin, The	B-36	162
Mary Alice Gnatzi-Knight	B-17	76
Mary Cary	B-17	25
Mary Lou	B-17	44
Mary Loy	?	172

NOSE ART NAME	AIRCRAFT TYPE	PAGE NUMBER
Snicklefritz	Jacket	78
Snootie Cutie	B-24	144
Snoozin' Suzan	B-17	69
Snow White and the Seven Dwarfs	B-24	114
Snugglebunny	B-29	182
Southern Belle	B-29	199
Southern Comfort	B-29	95
Southern Comfort	?	88
Southern Comfort	B-29	186
South Sea Sinner	B-29	106
Spare Parts	B-17	50
Sparky	B-17	50
Special Delivery	B-17	51
Special Delivery	B-29	200
Special Delivery	B-25	109
Spirit of '44	B-17	69
Squaw, The	B-24	145
Squeeze	B-24	83
Squeeze Play	B-29	179
Stage Door Canteen	B-17	69
Stag Party	B-17	51
Star Dust	B-17	51
Stars and Stripes	B-17	51
Stinky	B-17	51
Stormy Weather	B-24	154
Strange Cargo	B-29	180
Strawberry Bitch	B-24	104
Stric Nine	B-17	51
Stud	B-25	158
Stud Duck	B-17	69
Stuff	B-17	42
Sugar Puss	B-17	24
Sunkist Special	B-17	25
Sun Special	B-17	25
Superchief, The	B-24	149
Superman	B-17	70
Surprise Attack	B-24	12 & 83
Swamp Fire	B-17	52
Sweat and Pray	B-25	159
Sweater Girl, The	B-17	70
Sweater Girl	B-25	159
Sweat'er Out	B-17	77
Sweet Dish	B-17	52
Sweet Dreams	Jacket	77
Sweetest of Texas	B-24	127
Sweet Lorraine	B-25	159
Sweet'n Lola	B-29	194
Sweet Revenge	?	173
Swingin' on a Star	Jacket	77
Swoose, The	?	174
Swoose, The	B-26	164
Tag a Long	Jacket	78
Tail Wind	B-29	198
Tail Winds	B-24	145
Tale of Miss Fortune II	B-29	197
Tanaka Termite	B-29	180
Tantalizing Takeoff	Jacket	113
Tarfu	B-24	145
Target for Tonight	B-24	19
Target for Tonight	B-17	81
Target for Tonite	B-17	52
Taylor Maid	B-24	20
T.D.Y. Widow	B-29	196
Tempest Turner	B-17	52
Temptation	B-17	24
Temptation	B-24	145
Tennessee Belle	B-24	128
Tepee Time Gal	B-24	128
Texas Chubby	B-17	52
Texas Dol	B-29	199
Texas Gal	B-25	159
Texas Peace Maker	B-26	164
Texas Raiders	B-17	109
Thar She Blows	B-24	145
Thar She Blows III	B-24	145
That's "It"	B-29	195
There'll Always Be a Christmas	B-29	182
There's a Rainbow Round My Shoulder	?	169
This Above All	B-24	149
Three Feathers	B-29	194
Thumper	B-29	195
Thunderhead	B-29	176
Tiger Girl	B-17	52
Time'll Tell!	Jacket	78
Time's A Wastin	B-29	193
Times-A-Wastin	A-20	175
Tokyo Rose	B-29	195
Tom Paine	B-17	101
Tondelayo	B-17	70
Tondelayo	B-24	93
Toots	B-17	53
Tootsie	B-26	164
Top Secret	B-29	195
To Tokyo	B-29	53
Touch the Button Nell II	B-17	53
Tower of London	B-17	53
Tremlin' Gremlins	B-29	195
Tropical Trollop	B-24	146
Tropic Knight	B-24	114
T.S.	B-26	167
Turd Burd	B-17	53
Twang-g-g	Jacket	78
Twannggg	Jacket	78
Twan-n-g-g-g	B-17	53
Umbriago!	B-24	146
Uncle Sammy	B-17	54
Uncouth Bastard, The	B-17	70
Undecided	F-111	111
Under Ground Farmer	B-17	54
Uninvited, The	B-29	186
United Notions	B-29	182
Up an' Atom	B-29	195
USAFI	B-24	146
Valiant Virgin!	B-25	159
Veni-Vidi-Vici	Jacket	113
V-Grand 5000	B-24	136
Victory Girl	B-29	187
Victory Queen	B-17	70
Vikin's Vicious Virgin	B-25	156
Virgins Delight	B-17	54
Virgin Sturgeon	B-17	54
Virgin Vampire	B-24	146
Virgo	B-24	89
Visibility Perfect	Jacket	79
Vulgar Virgin, The	B-24	146
Wabash Cannonball	B-17	71

LIBRARY
OWENS COMMUNITY COLLEGE
P.O. BOX 10,000
TOLEDO, OHIO 43699